Forming Ministers for Whole-Community Faith Formation

Edited by

Janet Miller

Kathleen Truman

Katy Meister

Helen Keating

Resource Publications
San Jose, California

The Ministry Formation Sessions, Handouts, and Resource Sheets in this book first appeared in Celebrating The Lectionary, a whole-parish faith formation program published by Resource Publications. These texts were specially selected and edited for this book.

Reprint Department
Resource Publications, Inc.
160 E. Virginia St. #290
San Jose, CA 95112-5876
(408) 286-8505 voice
(408) 287-8748 fax

Library of Congress Cataloging in Publication Data

Forming ministers for whole-community faith formation / edited by Janet Miller,
    Kathleen Truman, Katy Meister, and Helen Keating.
        p.   cm.
        ISBN 0-89390-647-6
            1. Christian education of adults. 2. Catholic Church—Liturgy—Study and teaching.
            I. Miller, Janet I. II. Truman, Kathleen. III. Meister, Katy, 1974– .
            IV. Keating, Helen.

    BX921.F67   2006
    268'.434—dc22   2006048322

The Scripture quotations contained herein are taken or adapted from the New Revised Standard Version of the Bible: Catholic Edition © 1993 and 1989 by the Division of Christian Education of the National Council of the Churches of Christ in the U.S.A. Used by permission. All rights reserved.

Printed in the United States of America
06 07 08 09 10 | 5 4 3 2 1

Assistant Editor: Laura Quilling
Cover Design: Nelson Estarija

Contents

Paschal Mystery

Pentecost People

Appendix 2: Ministry Resource Sheets

Introduction

Forming Ministers for Whole-Community Faith Formation is a new kind of ministry manual for a fresh approach to community faith development. Because more adults are seeking formation, the movement is toward *integrated ministry.* In the past parishes implemented compartmentalized ministries — each having a specific job that rarely interfaced with other ministries. Catechists were *here*, liturgical ministries were *there*, community outreach was *elsewhere*, and the parish administration, support, and pastoral staff were entities unto themselves. Today, integrating ministry shifts the paradigm from isolation to collaboration.

Echoing a call from Vatican Council II for adult-centered faith formation, today's church leaders are strengthening the resolve to provide life-long formation in discipleship that is liturgically grounded and mission focused. Findings in the recent National Study on Youth and Religion show that the most powerful force affecting the faith lives of youth is the presence of faith-filled adults, adults whose faith practices serve as models and who immerse their families in the culture of a practicing community. More parishes realize that the future of the church is not just in the formation of children but also in the ongoing formation of adults who all — parents, aunts, uncles, grandparents, friends, and ministry leaders — take on catechetical roles in the community. This shift requires much more coordination, communication, and shared planning among ministry leaders.

In addition to training that provides ministers with mechanical ministry tools, parish ministers also need ongoing spiritual formation. Because the activities of the church are directed toward the liturgy and flow from its powers, the liturgical year is the natural source for faith formation (see *Constitution on the Sacred Liturgy* #10; from the documents of Vatican II). As we join in the eucharistic celebration and share the communal meal, we are called to become the bread broken and the cup poured out for others. All formation explores the meaning of this mystery on ever-deepening levels.

Spiritual formation — the integration of doctrine, morality, Scripture, sacramental life, mission, and service — is a life-long journey and part of the fiber of a believer's faith. This new paradigm is sometimes called the "praxis model," "lectionary-based or liturgical catechesis," "whole-community formation," or "life-long catechesis." It may be structured in a variety of formats: age-group meetings, weekly religion classes, whole-community intergenerational gatherings, youth groups, adult faith-sharing groups, or small Christian communities.

In this new model, the content of faith exploration comes from life experience in dialogue with Scripture, sacramental life, and the community of faith. Doctrinal and historical content meld with active participation in Jesus' mission of bringing about the reign of God. The sacramental life of the community nourishes and supports this mission as participants journey together through the liturgical year.

In the integrated ministry paradigm, every activity in the faith community provides opportunities for faith growth. Catechesis is not limited to classrooms, but every minister is a guide and facilitator of faith growth for each person touched in ministry. The goal is for the faithful not only to know *about* God but also to come to *know* God in very intimate relationships of transformative love. Ministers are codiscoverers on the journey as well as facilitators. Liturgists, presiders, and leaders of outreach and other groups all join with session catechists as faith formation ministers. We designed this ministry formation manual to provide support for all ministers to make the necessary transitions and integrate faith formation with the liturgical year. The four interactive sessions presented in this book are the foundation for well-formed ministers who will in turn implement integrated ministry for your whole-community faith formation.

Why Integrated, Liturgy-based Ministry?

The marriage of liturgy and catechesis can be traced through a number of church documents, starting with *On Evangelization in the Modern World* (*Evangelii Nuntiandi;* 1975). *The Rite of Christian Initiation of Adults* (1988) is a significant force in recognizing the power of liturgy to catechize and move seekers in hearts and minds along their faith journeys. Two key principles from the *General Directory for Catechesis* (1997) add to the momentum: first, that adult catechesis is the "axis" around which catechesis for all others revolves (#275), and second, that "catechesis is a responsibility of the entire Christian community" (#220), with the baptismal catechumenate model as the normative approach. In *Our Hearts Were Burning within Us: A Pastoral Plan for Adult Faith Formation in the United States* (1999), the U.S. bishops called for a new, multifaceted approach to adult formation that integrates catechesis in all areas of parish life, such as liturgy and family- and home-centered activities. Furthermore, *Catechism of the Catholic Church* #1074 says that liturgy is "the privileged place for catechizing the People of God," and the *National Directory for Catechesis* (2005) sums up the integral relationship of catechesis and liturgy by stating that sacramental practices come alive to avoid "hollow ritualism" and "intellectualized catechesis" through liturgy-based formation (#33).

Integrated ministry recognizes that the liturgy, with its cycles of word and sacrament, of being nurtured and sent forth, and of seasons and feasts, grounds life in the faith community. If you already began implementing integrated ministry, you know the excitement and the challenges inherent in this endeavor.

How to Use This Manual

This manual provides both the supporting background information and the practical tools needed to implement the paradigm of ongoing, liturgy-based faith formation and integrated ministry in your community. The practical tools are as follows:

- This Introduction contains information about integrated ministry for presentations to the parish board, pastor, parents, ministry leaders, and/or catechists.
- The "Directing Integrated Ministry" chapter explains the director's role, providing basics about integrated ministry, recruitment, formation, and support.
- Four fully planned sessions based on liturgical seasons (with options for years A, B, and C) combine theological information and practical implementation to form ministers in the context of the liturgical year. The stimulating experiences will prepare ministers to help facilitate faith formation in a multitude of faith community settings — as directors of spiritual quests, discipleship mentors, and presiders at prayer.
- Appendix 1 contains Formation Session Handouts to copy for use in the sessions. Each session's Preparation pages list the handouts for selected activities.
- Appendix 2 is a treasury of Ministry Resource Sheets on a variety of ministry topics. You may reproduce them to distribute as needed to whole-community faith formation leaders, catechists, the initiation team, youth leaders, lector trainers, and all other ministers who work with groups to facilitate faith development. Choose the topics that meet your ministers' needs, and create booklets or make individual copies to distribute as ongoing support. The session plans provide suggestions for using some of these handouts as well. Also find a template for ongoing evaluation; make several copies for each minister to use throughout the year.

Directing Integrated Ministry

Ministers of the faithful include those who accept roles of inviting and guiding others to grow spiritually. Ministers are those who lead or assist in Children's Liturgy of the Word, pre-school programs, children's catechesis, youth ministry, initiation and the catechumenate, adult faith-sharing groups, or sacramental preparation as well as all ministers of the word: proclaimers, homilists, and musicians who lead others in faith development.

Positions Defined

Develop job descriptions as a guide in recruiting, interviewing, and discernment. Keep them together in your own "book of ministry." Describe the skills needed for each ministry, the time commitment for gatherings, and the important time commitment to ongoing formation that the parish and diocese offer. Establish what the ministers will do for the faith community and what the faith community will do for the ministers. Help everyone understand that the ministers provide the time and talent while the faith community provides support and ongoing formation. Determine the term of each ministry, one year or shorter, with a discernment process before agreeing on renewal. Design a commitment form for each ministry based on the above information, and have each minister sign a copy at renewal.

The Recruitment of Formation Ministers

Recruiting ministers based on the catechumenate model is ongoing and invitational. In some ways, it is a year-round preoccupation for a director. Directors develop an eye for able people; in other words, directors wear "recruiting contact lenses" throughout the year. Encourage everyone involved in ministry to develop this eye and make suggestions. Offer potential ministers personal invitations, which is more effective than waiting for volunteers.

Utilize opportunities for recruitment by getting to know parishioners at community events. Take advantage of the mystagogy period for neophytes and the newly confirmed to extend invitations to become volunteers. Newcomers, the newly married, those graduating from high school, or those returning from college are good candidates for involvement in various ministries. Remember that the process of continual discernment is smoother than a last-minute recruitment crunch at the beginning of each season.

To get to know the gifts of potential leaders, invite new volunteers to help during sessions, in the office, or in adult and youth faith formation groups and during special events. Plan ministry positions for the volunteers in areas where each will succeed. For recruitment, focus on a person's skills instead of the need to fill ministry voids. Use a program such as the Spiritual Gifts Discernment Program from the Catherine of Siena Institute (www.siena.org) to discern the right ministry for each individual. Some people work better with small children, while others are great with teens or adults. Those who feel uncomfortable leading groups may help in a multitude of other ways, such as making phone calls, making copies, setting up prayer environments, or taking attendance.

Keep in mind that the director's role is to help each minister discern his or her own talents and to help everyone feel valued and welcome. The director is privileged to look on God's beloved ones and say, "This is good." The director has the God-given assignment to catch people doing what they do well. As the affirmer and namer of gifts, the director is a mirror that reflects the goodness and talents of others. One of the signs of true Christian community is the recognition of and flourishing of gifts.

Formation Sessions

When ministers come together for seasonal formation experiences, they start on the same page. The Holy Spirit sparks a transformation and unleashes the power of the paschal mystery inherent in liturgy to touch every area of parish life, family life, and ultimately, the world.

The *General Directory for Catechesis* calls for the coordination of all pastoral workers in Christian communities for integrated faith formation so the entire work of evangelization is consistent and so catechists are not isolated from the life of the community. This concept broadens the field of ministry formation in which all ministers who serve the faith community help form one another.

Imagine: What if lectors saw their role as proclaimers as an integral part of the faith formation process? What if parents were prepared ahead of time for what their children would experience, and what if they had materials and ideas for at-home connections? What if the pastor and homilists reflected with ministers of the community on key readings for the upcoming season? What if the parish council members were in tune with the concepts behind each season's service projects? The possibilities for deep transformation of parish life are limited only by the willingness of various groups to dialogue and cooperate. Invite! Invite! Invite!

In-depth interactive ministry formation sessions provide liturgical catechesis for all adults and youth who minister and help in the faith community in various ways. Those who participate will enjoy the benefits of unrushed community-building gathering time, faith-sharing reflection on seasonal Scripture, and prayer. All these elements are integral to the process and require a relaxed pace.

Prior to or at the beginning of each season, gather your formation leaders and other ministers. Because many programs follow the school-year model, the first formation session may occur in August or September. In the new paradigm, programs may begin with the liturgical year on the First Sunday of Advent; if so, hold the "Incarnation Season" session before the new liturgical year starts. Ongoing formation has no actual beginning or ending dates. If needed, consider implementing a new year-round schedule as a tangible sign of the new vision.

This manual offers the following formation sessions:

1. "Beginnings and Endings" (August or September) explores how we live our faith in Ordinary Time.

2. "Incarnation Season" (November, before Christ the King) prepares for Advent– Christmas.

3. "Paschal Mystery" (before Ash Wednesday) brings together the symbols of Lent and Easter.

4. "Pentecost People" (first week of Easter) develops how we live as people of the Spirit.

These four dynamic sessions provide the model to develop other sessions if you choose. For instance, you may want to hold a session for the beginning of Ordinary Time that focuses on the call to discipleship or one that prepares leaders for a summer program. See *FaithDays!* for preplanned intergenerational formation sessions (available from Resource Publications).

Ongoing Evaluation

With affirmation of gifts as the primary goal, regularly evaluating current ministers is as important as recruitment and formation. Throughout the year, find times to observe and name the gifts of each minister to create an atmosphere of positive reinforcement. Informally evaluate each minister by using walk-in visits and by assisting in special projects. Together the director and minister may periodically go over an evaluation form (see Appendix 2). Just as with recruitment, always focus on the gifts of the ministers and how they can best offer those gifts for the benefit of all.

Do not wait until the end of the year to discover or address problems. Frequent and varied evaluative encounters allow you to spot and address potential causes of frustration or if anyone is conveying faulty messages, allowing you to address problems in a timely and life-giving manner. Affirm God's value for each person so no one ever feels a sense of being rejected by God or the church.

Helping Prevent Burnout

As a program director, you have the joyful task of helping leaders fulfill the potential of their baptismal calls to ministry. Ministers need a sense of having an effect on the spiritual lives of those they lead. When people invest their lives in ministry efforts under your direction, they give gifts to the community and to you. Like flowers that offer great beauty in their fragileness, ministers who give of themselves need to be cared for and nourished.

Show appreciation with spontaneous notes of thanks or encouragement. If a minister is especially helpful to an individual, write a quick personal note to the person, and either hand deliver it or mail it (but do not send it with another person). Record birthdays and anniversaries on a calendar, and make arrangements for substitutes to free up ministers to celebrate important family events. Suggest prayer and journaling resources.

Burnout and frustration waste God's gifts to the church. As the ministry director, you can do much to alleviate the causes of burnout. Because ministers seldom give real reasons for leaving or for doing only the minimum, both of which are sure signs of burnout, communication requires more than ministers merely reporting what happens during gatherings.

Mutual support is vital, so structure opportunities for the ministers to share joys and frustrations. Gather together more than just for work or training. Offer miniretreats and provide other times for ministers to pray and reflect on their ministries and their faith. Encourage the expression of all feelings in life-giving ways. Listen and watch for clues to burnout, and address any negative symptoms by meeting privately with the person. See what you can offer to help alleviate concerns. Perhaps an assistant can relieve some pressure or share the preparation tasks. Sometimes a minister needs more affirmation, so point out the good you see. Because we are often blind to our own charisms, give voice to the goodness you see as if you were looking through God's eyes. Lavish genuine reinforcement on ministers to build self-confidence and enthusiasm.

Formation Sessions

Overview

The following segment offers four minister formation sessions: an orientation called "Beginnings and Endings," an introduction to Advent and Christmas called "Incarnation Season," an exploration of the mystery of Christ's life, death, and resurrection called "Paschal Mystery," and an examination of how we live as followers of Christ called "Pentecost People."

These sessions are designed to help ministers together deepen their liturgical spirituality to serve the faith community. Let all community ministers know the dates of the formation sessions, including lectors, catechists, potential substitutes, the Christian initiation team, the environment committee, hospitality and outreach people, musicians, deacons, priests, and other adults who serve the People of God.

The formation sessions are also planned for flexibility. For the option "Scripture and the Liturgical Season" in each session, choose the Scripture for the current year (A, B, or C). Select a variety of options for the other activities according to the needs of the ministers. Plan to offer different options in alternating years.

Go over the session, and choose activities from the suggested options. Then use the Preparation pages, which begin each session, to prepare for the sessions. Make copies of the Handouts in Appendix 1, which are specific to these sessions. The Resource Sheets in Appendix 2 are for general use and are sometimes recommended in the sessions.

Prepare a prayer center by covering a small table or other flat surface with a cloth in the liturgical color that reflects the season. Add a symbol of creation (such as flowers, a rock, or a branch) or a liturgical symbol (such as a cross, a saint picture, or oils), a candle, and a Bible. Plan to gather in the prayer space for prayer only, and move to another location for other activities. Allow ample time for prayer and building community. These segments help strengthen the ministry team and enhance their spirituality.

On the Preparation pages, the items in bold are things you need to bring for each activity. Sentences in bold in the sessions suggest wording for speaking to the group, but you may adapt this wording to your own speaking style. Sentences in regular print explain how to lead the group through the various activities. Adapt the sessions to the needs of the ministers in your community, using the suggestions as a spring-board and other activities as the Spirit moves you.

By participating in these sessions, the ministers in your community will enhance their own spirituality, build a support group, and form a chain of communication.

Beginnings and Endings
August or September: Orientation

FOCUS
To build community among ministers, with faith formation directed at Ordinary Time.

Materials Needed

GENERAL PREPARATION
- Invite all ministers — lectors, catechists, potential substitutes, the Christian initiation team, environment committee, hospitality and outreach people, musicians, deacons, priests, and other adults — to attend this faith formation experience.
- Ask the ministers to make a **list of supply needs** for this season.
- Bring **nametags** and **pens.**
- Locate the Handouts in Appendix 1 for specific options in this session and the Resource Sheets in Appendix 2 for general use.
- If some members prefer to pray in Spanish, see "Prayer Options" below.

GATHERING
- Cut **scrap paper** into 1-inch squares. Bring **small sheets of posterboard** and **glue.**
- Prepare the prayer space with a **green cloth, a Bible** opened to a Gospel reading for Fall Ordinary Time, **percussion instrument, candle,** and **fall leaves or flowers** in a **vase.** Bring **matches.** Set up **chairs** in a circle around the prayer space.
- *Prayer Options:* Consider using the bilingual prayers or copies of the **Resource Sheet "Liturgy of the Hours"** in Appendix 2 for Gathering and Missioning. Print the prayer on **newsprint or from a computer,** or display it on a **monitor.**

INTRODUCING THE SEASON
- Use the **Handout "Faith and Ordinary Time"** in Appendix 1 to prepare a presentation.

SCRIPTURE AND THE LITURGICAL SEASON
- *Year A: Age-Appropriate Dramatizations:* Use the **Handout "Breaking Open Scripture Year A: Matthew 16:21–27"** in Appendix 1. Ask 3 ministers to wear **simple costumes** and present "Jesus and Peter: A Drama." Ask 1 catechist for young children to tell the "Facial Expression Story." Copy Matthew 16:24b, 25, 26, and 27 on **4 separate small paper scrolls.** Roll and seal the scrolls, using **sealing wax, ribbon, or string.** Place the scrolls in a **shoebox,** and cover the scrolls with **sand.** Tightly seal the box with **tape,** and wrap it in **plain paper.** Plan to use the questions on the sheet to lead a discussion, or write the questions on **index cards** to distribute to leaders for small-group discussion.
- *Year B: Dramatization and Discussion:* Make copies of the **Handout "Breaking Open Scripture Year B: Mark 7:24–37"** in Appendix 1. Cut the columns apart. Give copies of "Drama: Jesus Listens and Heals" to 6 people to prepare to play the characters and copies of "Discussion Questions for Mark 7:24–31" to small-group discussion leaders.
- *Year C: Teachings of Jesus:* Use the **Handout "Breaking Open Scripture Year C: Luke 15–17"** in Appendix 1. Read these chapters in the Bible. Bring **Bibles** and **mustard seeds.** For small-group discussion, make copies of the Handouts for each leader (*optional*).
- *Faith Is …:* Make copies of the **Handout "Faith Is …"** in Appendix 1. Bring **pens.**
- *Break:* Ask families who participate in faith formation programs to prepare **snacks** and **beverages.**

Materials Needed

APPLICATION

Choose one or more of the following activities, varying the choices for each year of formation.

- *Scripture Faith Sharing:* Make copies of the **Handout "Scripture Sharing Sheet"** in Appendix 1.
- *Faith Action:* Make copies of the **Handout "Enabling Faith-in-Action"** in Appendix 1. Bring **newsprint.**
- *Household of Faith:* Make copies of the **Handout "Household of Faith"** in Appendix 1.
- *Faith Hand Signs:* Make copies of the **Handout "Faith Hand Signs"** in Appendix 1.
- *Successful Sessions:* Make copies of the **Handout "How Do I Know the Group Experience Is a Success?"** in Appendix 1.
- *God Speaks:* Bring a **portable audiocassette recorder** with **blank audiocassette tapes.** Plan a space apart from other groups. Bring **items that make interesting sounds** (such as musical instruments, a portable radio, or baby toys) (*optional*).
- *Prayer Environments:* From yard sales, clearance sales, and donations, accumulate items to use to set a prayer environment: a **variety of green, violet, and white cloth remnants, vases, candles, and dishes** (for holy water or oil). Gather **signs of creation** (such as interesting sticks, rocks, or shells) and **liturgical season items** (such as recycled rosaries, statues, or pictures). (*Note:* You can often find simple and inexpensive liturgical items hidden away in faith community cupboards, boxes, or basements. Check with the parish staff to make these little treasures available to ministers preparing prayer spaces for groups.) Have **small tables** available, or turn **sturdy boxes with lids** upside-down. (*Option:* Bring **small prizes.**)
- *Liturgy of the Hours Practice:* Make copies of the **Resource Sheet "Liturgy of the Hours"** in Appendix 2.
- *All Souls Intergenerational Prayer:* Make copies of the **Resource Sheet "All Souls Day Prayer"** in Appendix 2.
- *Catechizing Families:* Read and bring *National Catechetical Directory* #212 and *General Directory for Catechesis* #227 and #255.
- *Seasonal Music Sing-Along:* Bring **songbooks.** Invite **1 or more music ministers** to sing and/or play a **musical instrument.**

LAUNCHING THE SEASON

- Bring a **list of names and contact numbers for various ministries,** including room assignments and places each ministry group meets.
- Prepare to distribute copies of a **list of parish policies,** including policies on record-keeping and tracking attendance, use of restrooms, shared space, arrival and departure expectations, keys, meeting for prayer before sessions, cleanup policies, reimbursement procedures (if any), noise levels, the pastor's expectations, and how to obtain copies and materials.
- Make copies of the **Resource Sheet "Ongoing Evaluation Form"** in Appendix 2.
- Make copies of the **faith community calendar.**
- Plan the date for the "Incarnation Season" ministry formation session (before Advent).

MISSIONING

- Make copies of the **Resource Sheet "Minister's Prayer"** in Appendix 2. Cut apart.

MUSIC

- Bring a **CD/tape player, a CD/tape of reflective music,** and *Breaking Bread* **songbooks or music from liturgy.**
- Invite a **music minister** to lead the singing or play a **musical instrument.**

GATHERING

Welcome the ministers by name and offer nametags.

Mixer: Name Crossword Give each participant a set of 1-inch squares. Ask them each to print each letter of their names on separate squares. Form groups of six people gathered around the small sheets of posterboard. The groups work cooperatively to compile a crossword using the letters of their names (if needed, they can add last names). They glue the letters in place. Each group introduces its members to the larger group using the posters.

Gathering Prayer Call the ministers to prayer by striking the percussion instrument. With a hand motion, invite everyone to sit in a circle in the prayer space. Light the candle.

> **The Scriptures, God's holy word, tell us to listen and hear. Sometimes talking to God is easy, and sometimes it is difficult. Let go and let God speak to us.**
>
> - **How do you think God speaks to us? (*Affirm responses.*)**
>
> **God speaks to us in a variety of ways: Sometimes it is in liturgy; other times God speaks through nature; and sometimes God speaks through other people. God speaks through the Scriptures, and God speaks most clearly through Jesus.**
>
> **I will play some quiet music. Listen to what the music tells you about God.**

Play reflective music.

> - **What did you discover about God as you listened? (*Affirm responses.*)**
>
> **Listening to music can be one form of prayer. Anything we do becomes a prayer when it leads us to God. Name something you do every day that you might turn into a prayer by simply thinking about God while you do it.**

If needed, mention that *Ephphatha* means "Be open." Ask the members to respond "Ephphatha" (*ef-fa-tha*) for each of the following expressions:

> **O Jesus, touch our eyes and say, *"Ephphatha."***
> **O Jesus, touch our ears and say, *"Ephphatha."***
> **O Jesus, touch our minds and say, *"Ephphatha."***
> **O Jesus, touch our hearts and say, *"Ephphatha."***
> **Be with us, O Jesus, as we seek to know you more clearly, love you more dearly, and serve you more fully.**
> **We pray through your Holy Spirit, one God forever. Amen.**

Sing "All Are Welcome" from *Breaking Bread* or a song from liturgy

Prayer Options For bilingual prayer, say the following prayer:

> **Nosotros somos su pueblo. / We are God's people.**
>
> **Nosotros somos ovejas de su rebaño. / We are the sheep of God's flock.**
>
> **Te damos gracias y te bendecimos, Dios. / We praise you and bless you, God.**
>
> **Tú tienes las palabras de vida eterna. / You have the words of everlasting life. Amen.**

For evening prayer, light a candle and incense. Begin with an opening prayer, hymn, and psalm. The reading will take place during the session (see the Resource Sheet "Liturgy of the Hours").

Extinguish the candle.

INTRODUCING THE SEASON

Introduce the season of Ordinary Time using the Handout "Faith and Ordinary Time." If this session occurs at another time of the year instead of fall, adapt the following:

> **Fall is a time of beginnings and endings. Many catechetical programs begin during September. We bring new members onto our teams, and we welcome new participants to our sessions. We end any summer programs. We wind down the liturgical year as Ordinary Time ends and leads us to begin anew at Advent.**
>
> **The word "ordinary" means "in order" or "using ordinal numbers to count the Sundays." "Ordinary" also means "usual, commonplace, or customary." We sanctify that which is usually of little notice by giving it our attention. We follow Jesus, the master of presenting the ordinary in ways that gave new vision to listeners. We accept the challenge to see the holy in each person we meet.**
>
> **Special liturgical feasts take precedence when they land on a Sunday: the Exaltation of the Holy Cross, the Commemoration of the Faithful Departed, and the Lateran Basilica. During October, we celebrate the Rosary, Right to Life Sunday, and Mission Sunday. We also celebrate a type of triduum beginning on All Hallows Eve, rising on All Saints Day, and culminating on All Souls Day.**

SCRIPTURE AND THE LITURGICAL SEASON

Use copies of the Handout "Breaking Open Scripture ..." for the current liturgical year (A, B, or C) with one of the first three options below to help the ministers (catechists, lectors, preachers, and others) enter the experience of the word.

Year A: Age-Appropriate Dramatizations The participants present and explore Matthew 16:14–27 using the two methods on the Handout "Breaking Open Scripture Year A: Matthew 16:14–27." For "Jesus and Peter: A Drama," three presenters wear simple costumes. Have the sandbox containing scrolls with Scripture verses handy. For "Facial Expression Story," the other presenter uses an approach for small children as described on the sheet. After both presentations, form small groups, or discuss the following together:

- **For which age levels is each way of presenting the Scripture appropriate?**
- **What are the advantages of presenting Scripture in different ways?**
- **What other ways might you present Scripture stories?**
- **What adaptations might be necessary for the ages, ethnicities, and cultural interests in our community?**
- **What other needs do we seek to meet?**

Year B: Dramatization and Discussion Using copies of the Handout "Breaking Open Scripture Year B: Mark 7:24–37," six participants present the drama. Form small groups to discuss the Gospel using "Discussions Questions for Mark 7:24–31." Gather the larger group, and together form some conclusions such as the following:

- Jesus' ability to recognize the faith of non-Jewish people was a shift away from the ancient tradition of his culture, in which only Jews were thought to hold true faith. Jesus became aware of his healing power after listening to the pleas of the woman.
- Words can carry a lot of power to hurt or heal. Words that discourage or insult can cause hurt. Words that are honest, that encourage, and that comfort can bring healing.
- In the upcoming week, be aware of the words you hear. Notice which ones promote healing and which ones carry the power to hurt. Resolve to use words that heal.

Year C: Teachings of Jesus Distribute Bibles. Use the Handout "Breaking Open Scripture Year C: Luke 15–17" to help the ministers recall some of Jesus' teachings in Luke's Gospel. Have mustard seeds handy. (*Option:* Form small groups, distributing a copy of the Handout to each group leader.)

Faith Is ... Distribute copies of the Handout "Faith Is ..." and pens. Give the group a few minutes to read the sheet and complete the statements. Discuss the following questions:

- **How does your faith statement reflect your faith experience?**
- **What does your faith statement say about your image of God?**
- **What does it mean to be faithful?**
- **Who has faith in you?**
- **What can you share with those you have come to nurture?**

Break Offer the snacks and beverages prepared by families who participate in faith formation programs.

APPLICATION

When ministers work together to prepare for the season, we grow through the sharing of ideas and build community among the ministerial team and faith community leaders. Choose one or more of the following options.

Scripture Faith Sharing Lectors, deacons, priests, catechists, and other ministers meet together or in small groups. Choose from readings for the season, and distribute copies of the Handout "Scripture Sharing Sheet" to share insights and develop session or homily ideas.

Faith Action Distribute copies of the Handout "Enabling Faith-in-Action." Review the sheet. On newsprint brainstorm actions the group might do. Have people pick topics and form small groups with others with similar interests. Challenge each group to create an action plan.

Household of Faith Distribute copies of the Handout "Household of Faith," and read the information together. Ask the following questions:

- **Through which of these doors did you enter?**
- **Do you know people who came to their faith by different ways?**
- **What do you think "Faith is a journey — not a destination" means?**
- **How many people do you think experience times of doubt and questioning?**

Jesus' disciples faced a lot of challenges as they tried to live the way Jesus taught. Sometimes they felt unsure that they had enough faith to do what Jesus asked.

Faith Hand Signs Distribute copies of the Handout "Faith Hand Signs." Invite the participants to learn the hand signs, and practice them together for faith sharing.

Successful Sessions Distribute copies of the Handout "How Do I Know the Group Experience Is a Success?" Allow the ministers time to review the sheet. Then review it together and discuss why the "a" answers stimulate faith growth more than the "b" responses.

God Speaks Provide an audiocassette recorder and tapes. Designate a space apart from the others for this activity. Invite the participants to record sounds in various places. Bring items that make interesting sounds (*optional*). Invite the group to share their recordings while the others guess the sounds. Reflect together on how God speaks through sounds.

Prayer Environments Display items such as green, violet, and white cloth remnants, candles, dishes; signs of creation (greenery, flowers, rocks, driftwood); and liturgical symbols (oils, bread, wine, saint pictures, Marian objects). Invite all to create interesting prayer spaces with the materials. (*Option:* Hold a contest, with the other participants judging. Everyone wins a prize and may keep articles of choice for prayer spaces for sessions or home use.)

Liturgy of the Hours Practice Distribute copies of the Resource Sheet "Liturgy of the Hours." Practice leading the others in prayer.

All Souls Intergenerational Prayer Distribute copies of the Resource Sheet "All Souls Day Prayer." Discuss how and when various groups in the faith community might join together for this prayer. If the participants decide to lead this prayer experience for the faith community, form groups now. Assign responsibilities for planning and leading the service.

Catechizing Families Read #212 in *National Catechetical Directory* and #227 and #255 in *General Directory for Catechesis*. Discuss whole-family and whole-community catechesis. Brainstorm ways to offer intergenerational faith experiences for the community.

Seasonal Music Sing-Along Distribute songbooks. Music minister(s) work with the group to choose songs for liturgy and catechesis for Fall Ordinary Time. (*Option:* Catechists may arrange for musicians to attend some sessions to pray and practice songs.)

LAUNCHING THE SEASON

- Distribute copies of the parish policies, and review together. Answer questions (making a note of any questions that the parish staff or pastor need to clarify, and get back to the people with questions as soon as possible). Emphasize the policies for using the copier, telephones, and the staff office and for requesting copies.
- Distribute copies of the faith community calendar. Note when events or programs begin, including upcoming faith community events that require ministry collaboration. Discuss special days. Consider celebrations of Rosh Hashanah and Yom Kippur for interfaith appreciation. Talk about the fall triduum celebration beginning on All Hallows Eve, rising on All Saints Day, and culminating in All Souls Day.
- Ask if anyone needs help, and make appointments to meet with those members soon. Distribute copies of the Resource Sheet "Ongoing Evaluation Form," and suggest that they make copies and use the form to evaluate their own ministries periodically.
- Determine what special supplies the ministers will need for fall programs, and stock the supply closet accordingly.
- Review where to find sets of Bibles and songbooks and the checkout policy.
- Distribute lists of names and contact numbers for the various ministries and room assignments for activities.
- Give the date for the ministry formation session "Incarnation Season," which will occur before Advent begins.

MISSIONING

Gather in the prayer space. Distribute copies of the Resource Sheet "Minister's Prayer, and pray together. Encourage the ministers to retain the sheet to use during personal prayer.

Sing "All That Is Hidden" from *Breaking Bread* or a song from liturgy

(*Option:* If extra items are left over from the prayer environment activity, invite the ministers to choose one symbol to use in prayer.)

Closing Prayer Options For bilingual prayer, say the following:

> **O God, show us how to practice justice and love.**
> **A llevar tu paz a aquéllos que están angustiados.**
>
> **Help us forgive those who hate us and give them peace.**
> **Haznos instrumentos de tu palabra.**
>
> **Renew our hearts to show the world that you really live in our hearts.**
> **Gracias por tu presencia y amor. Amen.**

For evening prayer, close with the appropriate canticle, intercessions, and Our Father.

Incarnation Season
November: Preparing for Advent–Christmas

FOCUS
To lead ministers in the faith community into the incarnation season.

Materials Needed ✎

GENERAL PREPARATION

■ Invite all ministers — lectors, catechists, potential substitutes, the Christian initiation team, environment committee, hospitality and outreach people, musicians, deacons, priests, and other adults — to attend this faith formation experience.

■ Ask the ministers to make a **list of supply needs** for this season.

■ Bring **nametags** and **pens.**

■ Locate the Handouts in Appendix 1 for specific options in this session and the Resource Sheets in Appendix 2 for general use.

■ If some members prefer to pray in Spanish, see "Prayer Options" below.

GATHERING

■ Bring **small gifts,** one for each participant, for the upcoming season (something little such as holy cards or violet votive candles). Wrap all the gifts together in several **layers of wrapping paper** and **boxes of graduated sizes.** Set up **chairs** in a circle.

■ Prepare the prayer space with a **violet cloth, a Bible** opened to a Gospel reading for the season, and an **Advent wreath or candle.** Bring **matches.** Ask a participant to lead the Gathering Prayer.

■ *Prayer Options:* Consider using the bilingual prayers or copies of the **Resource Sheet "Liturgy of the Hours"** in Appendix 2 for Gathering and Missioning. Print the prayer on **newsprint or from a computer,** or display it on a **monitor.**

INTRODUCING THE SEASON

■ Read and make copies of the **Handout "Seasons Merge"** in Appendix 1. Plan to introduce the seasons of Advent and Christmas, including symbols and signs.

SCRIPTURE AND THE LITURGICAL SEASON

■ *Year A: Small-Group Discussion:* Make copies of the **Handout "Breaking Open Scripture Year A: Matthew 24:37–44 and Matthew 3:13–17"** in Appendix 1. Bring **Bibles.**

■ *Year B: Exploring "Expectation":* Make copies of the **Handout "Breaking Open Scripture Year B: Mark 13:33–37"** in Appendix 1.

■ *Year C: Kinesthetic Proclamation:* Make copies of the **Handout "Breaking Open Scripture Year C: When Jesus Comes Again"** in Appendix 1.

■ *Incarnation: The Manger Means Justice:* Make copies of the **Handout "The Manger Means Justice"** in Appendix 1.

■ *Break:* Ask families who participate in faith formation programs to prepare and serve **snacks** and **beverages.**

<table>
<tr><td>

Materials Needed

</td></tr>
</table>

APPLICATION

Choose one or more of the following activities, varying the choices for each year of formation.

- *Scripture Faith Sharing:* Make copies of the **Handout "Scripture Sharing Sheet"** (from "Beginnings and Endings") in Appendix 1. Bring **lectionaries or proclaimer workbooks.**
- *Jesse Tree Ornaments:* Bring **Bibles.** Make copies of the **Handout "Jesse Tree"** in Appendix 1. Bring a **wide variety of craft supplies** (including clay, straw, cotton balls, glitter, fur and other fabrics, toothpicks, shiny paper, glue, and card stock) and **small storage containers.**
- *John the Baptist:* Bring **Bibles** and **drawing supplies.**
- *Blessing Table Tents:* Bring **recycled Christmas cards, scissors, rulers, glue, card stock, craft knives with protective surfaces,** and **fine-tipped markers.** Make arrangements to deliver the table tents to local care homes.
- *Making Advent Wreaths:* Make copies of the **Handout "Advent Wreath"** in Appendix 1. Bring an assortment of materials to make wreaths: **violet and rose taper candles; white candles; violet ribbon; craft knives or good scissors; craft putty; glue; thumbtacks; fire-safe greenery; 12-inch donut-type circles of foam or heavy cardboard; self-drying clay; 12-by-2-inch pieces of wood** (predrill holes according to the instructions on the Handout, or bring **drills** and **bits); small glass jars with small violet, rose or pink, and white votive candles;** and **heavy, disposable circular trays.**
- *Magi Gifts:* Make copies of the **Handout "Magi Gifts"** in Appendix 1.
- *Rite of Acceptance:* If your community is preparing to celebrate a rite of acceptance, plan how various ministers can help prepare, including greeting and praying for the catechumens.
- *Seasonal Music Sing-Along:* Invite **1 or more music ministers** to sing and/or play a **musical instrument,** preparing songs that will be part of liturgy during the Incarnation season. Bring **songbooks.** (*Option:* Ask if the music ministers are willing to visit the faith formation sessions to practice with children and other participants.)

LAUNCHING THE SEASON

- Review and prepare to distribute copies of a **list of parish policies,** including policies on the use of restrooms, shared space, arrival and departure expectations, meeting for prayer before sessions, cleanup policies, noise levels, and the pastor's expectations.
- Make copies of the **faith community calendar** with the schedule of seasonal activities. Plan when the groups will meet during the holidays, including special days and holy days that ministers may want to incorporate in their sessions or homilies.
- Plan to discuss having a whole-community Advent reconciliation service.
- Make copies of the **Resource Sheet "Ongoing Evaluation Form"** in Appendix 2.
- Plan the date for the "Paschal Mystery" ministry formation session (before Lent).

MISSIONING

- Bring **incense or incense with charcoal in a heat-proof container** and **matches.** Make copies of the **Resource Sheet "Family Healing Prayer"** in Appendix 2. Use a **highlighter marker** to highlight a different sentence on each sheet. Plan to give the sheets to volunteers to prepare to read.

MUSIC

- Bring a **CD/tape player, a CD/tape of peppy music,** and *Breaking Bread* songbooks, *Rise Up And Sing* Second Edition (Oregon Catholic Press), or **music from liturgy.**
- Invite a **music minister** to lead the singing or play a **musical instrument.**

GATHERING

Welcome the ministers by name and offer nametags. When all the participants arrive, invite them to sit in a circle. Introduce anyone new to the group.

Mixer: Gift Game To start the game, give the wrapped box to one person. Have the participants pass the box while you play peppy music. Stop the music after several moments. The person with the gift at that moment says her or his name and removes a piece of wrapping paper. Start the music again, and continue this cycle until the participants remove all the layers of paper. The participant who removes the last layer shares the gifts with everyone.

Gathering Prayer Gather everyone in the prayer area. Light the candle or a candle in an Advent wreath. Teach the response "We watch in hope."

> **Watching for signs of your reign, (*response*).**
> **Watching for you to come again, (*response*).**
> **Watching while we continue your work, (*response*).**
> **Come now, O God of hope.**
> **We watch; we wait, and we prepare for Jesus, who lives and reigns forever.**
> **Amen.**

Ask the participants to open their songbooks.

Sing "O Come, Divine Messiah" from *Breaking Bread,* "Prepare The Way" from *Rise Up And Sing,* or a song from liturgy

Prayer Options For bilingual prayer, display the following prayer on newsprint, a computer display, or printout. Invite those who know Spanish to read the Spanish lines and the others to read the English lines.

> **Ven, Salvador, ven. Libra fieles todos.**
> **Come, O Savior. Set your people free.**
>
> **Oh, Jesús, ven a mí con santo amor.**
> **O Jesus, come, come with holy love.**
>
> **Dulce redentor, ven, no tardes en llegar y la paz al mundo le daras.**
> **Come, sweet redeemer, bring peace to all the world.**

For evening prayer, light a candle and incense. Begin with an opening prayer, hymn, and psalm. The reading will take place during the session (see the Resource Sheet "Liturgy of the Hours").

Extinguish any candles.

INTRODUCING THE SEASON

The Seasons Introduce the seasons of Advent and Christmas. Use the Handout "Seasons Merge" for information about the Advent season and its symbols and signs.

> When we watch for something or someone, we feel excited, anxious, nervous, and happy. During this first week of Advent, we are aware that the most important person we watch for is Jesus.
>
> We minister during Advent with a threefold purpose: We prepare to celebrate Jesus born among us; we prepare for Jesus' second coming; and we prepare for Jesus' ongoing birth in each of our hearts. For three Sundays during Christmastime, we celebrate that Jesus came to be one with us. Today we will explore the Gospel reading for the First Sunday of Advent and prepare for this wonderful time of year.

Distribute copies of the Handout "Seasons Merge."

SCRIPTURE AND THE LITURGICAL SEASON

Use copies of the Handout "Breaking Open Scripture …" for the current liturgical year (A, B, or C) with one of the first three options below to help the ministers (catechists, lectors, preachers, and others) enter the incarnation season.

Year A: Small-Group Discussion Form small groups and distribute Bibles. Have the groups use the Handout "Breaking Open Scripture Year A: Matthew 24:37–44 and Matthew 3:13–17" to read, discuss, and prepare for the season.

Year B: Exploring "Expectation" Show the hand sign, and ask the participants to imitate the sign and say, "Watch." Use two fingers to form a "V." Point them under your eyes, and flip the fingers outward. Have them plan to use this hand sign when you proclaim the Gospel. Using the hand sign at the appropriate spots, proclaim Mark 13:33–37 from the Bible. Distribute copies of the Handout "Breaking Open Scripture Year B: Mark 13:33–37," and form small groups to discuss the questions. Ask the group to think about one thing they can do as they watch with expectation for Jesus' second coming and the completion of God's just reign. Invite those who wish to share one idea.

Year C: Kinesthetic Proclamation Invite the members to sit so they can see a sheet in front of them but have their hands free. Distribute copies of the Handout "Breaking Open Scripture Year C: When Jesus Comes Again." Encourage them to read it aloud together and do the motions. Form small groups to discuss the questions. Ask each group to report on one of the questions, rotating questions so that you cover all of them.

Second Coming Guide a discussion about the second coming using the following:

- **What have you heard about Jesus' second coming?**
- **What feelings do you have about the final coming of Jesus?**
- **What can we do to look forward to the coming with hope, wonder, and joy instead of fear?**

Ministering during the seasons of Advent and Christmas presents a particular challenge. The Advent season ideally focuses on the themes of waiting and hope, and the nativity story is not told until Christmas. Children and even many adults may need more preparation for Christmas by learning the story earlier. Also, if you wait until the last Sunday of Advent to tell the Christmas story, many people will not hear it because of family trips (or suspended sessions).

Incarnation: The Manger Means Justice Together explore the meaning of "incarnation." Form small groups. Distribute copies of the Handout "The Manger Means Justice." Ask the participants to read the information and discuss the questions. For shared wisdom, ask each group to share one thing they can do as a response to Jesus in the manger calling us to justice.

Break Offer the snacks and beverages prepared by families who participate in faith formation programs.

APPLICATION

When ministers work together to prepare for the season, we grow through the sharing of ideas and build community among the ministerial team and faith community leaders. Choose one or more of the following options.

Scripture Faith Sharing Lectors, deacons, priests, catechists, and other ministers meet together or in small groups, look through lectionaries or proclaimer workbooks, and choose from readings for the season. They might use the Handout "Scripture Sharing Sheet" from the "Beginnings and Endings" session as a guide to develop and share insights.

Jesse Tree Ornaments Distribute copies of the Handout "Jesse Tree," and use it as a guide to read the passages in Bibles. Use a variety of craft supplies to develop ornaments with symbols based on the Scripture. For instance, for Ruth, someone may use a bunch of wheat. Someone might use an animal skin for Rebecca. Have the participants place their ornaments in small storage containers.

John the Baptist Distribute Bibles and read about John the Baptist (Year A: Matthew 3:1–12 and 11:2–11; Year B: Mark 1:1–8 and John 1:6–8,19–28; Year C: Luke 3:1–6,10–18). The ministers draw what they think John the Baptist looked like or make an emblem to represent John. Those who wish may share their images with the larger group.

Blessing Table Tents Using recycled Christmas cards, scissors, rulers, glue, pieces of card stock, craft knives with protective surfaces, and fine-tipped markers, the participants make table or tray tents with a seasonal picture on one side and a table blessing written on the other. You will distribute the table tents at local care homes. Choose some participants to make deliveries.

Making Advent Wreaths Invite the ministers to make Advent wreaths to use in faith formation sessions, for home use, or to give to a care facility. Distribute copies of the Handout "Advent Wreath." Have the participants choose from the various materials and create Advent wreaths.

Magi Gifts Form small groups. Distribute copies of the Handout "Magi Gifts," and have the groups reflect on the meaning of Jesus' epiphany. Each group shares one insight with the larger group.

Rite of Acceptance If the rite of acceptance will occur in your faith community during this season, have the ministers suggest ways other faith formation groups may participate and offer catechumens support (such as greeting and praying for them, being sponsors, meeting occasionally for refreshments, presentations, or discussion). Make plans accordingly.

Seasonal Music Sing-Along Introduce the music minister(s) who will lead. Distribute songbooks. Have the group practice singing music from liturgy for the upcoming liturgical seasons. Encourage the ministers to use some of this music with their groups to prepare participants for worship. (*Option:* Plan times for a music minister to visit the sessions to practice with the participants.) As a group, decide if all of the levels will meet for a whole-community Christmas carol party or other parish event (such as Our Lady of Guadalupe, St. Nicholas, or St. Lucia celebrations). If so, make the arrangements for the date, space, refreshments, publicity, and musicians.

LAUNCHING THE SEASON

- Review the parish policies as needed.
- Distribute copies of the faith community calendar for the Advent and Christmas seasons. Discuss ways that children, youth, and adults of the faith community will be encouraged to participate in events.
- Together discuss how various programs the faith community offers will be coordinated, including timing and use of space to set up and get ready for the events.
- Discuss how to incorporate special holy days and holidays into ministry. Consider the feasts of the Immaculate Conception, Our Lady of Guadalupe, the Holy Innocents, Anniversary of the Massacre at Wounded Knee, Jewish and Muslim holy days, and Kwanzaa.
- Share ideas about "gifting" helpers and participants for Christmas in nonmaterialistic ways.
- Discuss a faith community reconciliation service and how the catechetical groups will participate.
- For those who want ongoing Scripture faith sharing, plan times for the ministers to meet for regular faith sharing based on the Scriptures.
- Discuss any problems anyone has encountered. Ask if anyone feels the need for additional help, and make an appointment to meet with them. Ask if anyone needs a copy of the Resource Sheet "Ongoing Evaluation Form," and suggest that they make copies and use the form to evaluate their own ministries periodically.
- Ask for the ministers' supply lists of materials they will need for Advent and Christmas sessions, and replenish the supply closet.
- Give the date for the ministry formation session "Paschal Mystery," which will occur before Lent begins.

MISSIONING

Gather in the prayer space. Light the incense and candles. Have the prepared volunteers read from copies of the Resource Sheet "Family Healing Prayer," which is appropriate for group prayer on the feast of the Holy Family. Then solemnly incense the ministers.

Sing "Advent Lamb of God" from *Breaking Bread* or a bilingual Advent song such as "O Come, O Come, Emmanuel/O Ven, O Ven, Emanuel"

Closing Prayer Options For bilingual prayer, say the following:

Todos están parados en un circulo.
Diga a la persona próxima hasta que cada uno recibe el mensaja:
"Te acompañan Dios y todos los angeles."

We will all stand in a circle.
Say the following to the person on your left until everyone receives the message:
"God goes with you, God and all the angels."

For evening prayer, close with the appropriate canticle, intercessions, and Our Father.

Paschal Mystery
January or February: Preparing for Lent

FOCUS
To reflect together as ministers of this community about how our Lenten journeys leads us deeper into the paschal mystery.

Materials Needed
✎

GENERAL PREPARATION

■ Invite all ministers — lectors, catechists, potential substitutes, the Christian initiation team, environment committee, hospitality and outreach people, musicians, deacons, priests, and other adults — to attend this faith formation experience.

■ Ask the ministers to make a **list of supply needs** for this season.

■ Bring **nametags** and **pens.**

■ Locate the Handouts in Appendix 1 for specific options in this session and the Resource Sheets in Appendix 2 for general use.

■ If some members prefer to pray in Spanish, see "Prayer Options" below.

GATHERING

■ Bring **clipboards or other hard surfaces for writing** and **paper.**

■ Prepare the prayer space with a **violet cloth, candle, crucifix,** and a **Bible** opened to a Gospel reading from Lent. Cut **violet construction paper** into 1-by-9-inch strips, and place them on the prayer cloth. Bring **pens, a stapler or tape, a percussion instrument,** and **matches.**

■ *Prayer Options:* Consider using the bilingual prayers or copies of the **Resource Sheet "Liturgy of the Hours"** in Appendix 2 for Gathering and Missioning. Make copies of the **Resource Sheet "Bilingual Prayers for Lent"** in Appendix 2. Divide the prayer for Gathering and Missioning, using the session content as the Scripture element.

INTRODUCING THE SEASON

■ Plan a presentation based on the **Handout "Paschal Mystery Background Information"** in Appendix 1.

■ Bring **index cards, pens, newsprint,** and **markers.**

SCRIPTURE AND THE LITURGICAL SEASON

■ *Year A: Tempting:* Bring **Bibles, a freshly baked loaf of bread, a platter,** and a **cloth.** Ask a reader to prepare to proclaim Matthew 4:1–11 from the **Bible.** Make copies of the **Handout "Breaking Open Scripture Year A: Matthew 4:1–11"** in Appendix 1.

■ *Year B: Guided Meditation:* Arrange for a carpeted area where you can dim the lights, if possible. Write the discussion questions in the session on **index cards,** and give them to leaders for small-group discussion. Practice the **Handout "Breaking Open Scripture Year B: Mark 1:12–15"** in Appendix 1.

■ *Year C: In the Desert:* Bring **Bibles, rocks, a cactus, an empty water bottle,** and a **grocery bag.** Practice the **Handout "Breaking Open Scripture Year C: Jesus in the Desert"** in Appendix 1 as a guide to tell Luke 4:1–13. For small-group discussion, print the questions in "Desert Experience" in the session on **index cards.**

■ *Metanoia and the Church:* Make copies of the **Handout "Conversion: A Church Task"** in Appendix 1. (*Option:* Bring copies of *Dogmatic Constitution on the Church* [*Lumen Gentium*]).

■ *Break:* Ask families who participate in faith formation programs to prepare and serve **snacks** and **beverages.**

**Materials
Needed**

APPLICATION

Choose one or more of the following activities, varying the choices for each year of formation.

■ *Scripture Faith Sharing:* Make copies of the **Handout "Scripture Sharing Sheet"** (from "Beginnings and Endings") in Appendix 1. Bring **lectionaries or proclaimer workbooks.**

■ *Lenten and Easter Symbols:* Set up a display with **violet, red, and white cloths, budding branches, desert plants, sand in a container, nails, crown of thorns, pretzels, bread, wine, ashes in a container, stones, a plain cross, Passion cross, a resurrection cross, spring flowers (Easter lilies, if available), an Easter egg, floating candle arrangements,** and **Easter breads.**

■ *Palm Cross Instructions:* Make copies of the **Handout "Palm Cross Instructions"** in Appendix 1. Set out **rulers, scissors,** and **construction paper.**

■ *Temptations in the Mall:* Bring **scratch paper** and **props.** (*Option:* Bring **examples of magazine articles and advertisements, movies,** and **songs.**)

■ *Mission Support:* Make copies of the **Handout "Mission Support"** in Appendix 1. Arrange to use a **computer with internet access** in an office space, or e-mail the participants to ask them to bring **handheld computers with internet access.**

■ *The Scrutinies:* Make copies of the **Handout "The Scrutinies"** in Appendix 1.

■ *The Stations for Today:* Make copies of the **Handout "Stations for Today"** in Appendix 1. Set up an outdoor area for the stations, possibly with **pictures of people suffering in the world,** or arrange to use the church display of the stations.

■ *Reconciliation Service:* Make copies of the **Handout "Community Reconciliation Service"** in Appendix 1. Bring **supplies to make posters.**

■ *Seasonal Music Sing-Along:* Invite **1 or more music ministers** to sing and/or play a **musical instrument,** preparing songs that will be part of liturgy during this season. Bring **songbooks.** (*Option:* Ask if the music ministers are willing to visit the faith formation sessions to practice with children and other participants.)

LAUNCHING THE SEASON

■ Review and prepare to distribute copies of a **list of parish policies,** including policies on record-keeping and tracking attendance, use of restrooms, shared space, arrival and departure expectations, keys, meeting for prayer before sessions, cleanup policies, noise levels, reimbursement procedures (if any), the pastor's expectations, office use, and how to obtain copies and materials.

■ Make copies of the **faith community calendar** with the schedule of liturgies for the Triduum and events for the Elect.

■ Make copies of the **Resource Sheet "Ongoing Evaluation Form"** in Appendix 2.

■ Plan the date for the "Pentecost People" ministry formation session (near the end of Lent or the beginning of the Easter season).

MISSIONING

■ Bring **fragrant oil** in a **votive candleholder.** (*Option:* For a large number of participants, bring 2 votive candleholders, and plan for two people to anoint in two directions.)

MUSIC

■ Bring a **CD/tape player, a CD/tape of reflective music,** and *Breaking Bread* **songbooks or music from liturgy.**

■ Invite a **music minister** to lead the singing or play a **musical instrument.**

GATHERING

Welcome the ministers by name and offer nametags.

Mixer: Listen to One Another Assign pairs. Give each pair a piece of paper on a clipboard and a pencil. Have the pairs sit back to back. Explain that one person draws only what the other partner, the "director," describes. Caution the "directors" not to reveal the item while giving directions. Without looking at the pictures, have the directors tell the group what they described, and have the partners reveal the pictures. Discuss the importance of clearly saying what we want others to understand and listening to understand what others are saying.

Gathering Prayer Call the ministers to prayer by striking the percussion instrument. Light the candle.

> **Jesus models praying as a way to gain strength against temptation. During Lent we expand the ways we pray to lead us deeper into the paschal mystery. Think for a moment about others who need our prayers.**

On slips of violet paper, have the participants write down their prayer intentions. Using a stapler or tape, construct a prayer chain by looping the strips through one another to form links. Place the prayer chain on the prayer cloth, and invite those who wish to offer intentions aloud. After each, all respond, "Jesus of our journey, strengthen those in need."

After the intentions, conclude with the following:

> **O divine Spirit, come upon all of us gathered here. Help us to lead your people on the journey toward you. Guide us this Lenten season away from temptation. Make us willing to do your will. One God forever. Amen.**

Sing "This Season Calls Us" from *Breaking Bread* or a song from liturgy

Prayer Options For bilingual prayer, distribute copies of the Resource Sheet "Bilingual Prayers for Lent." Ask the participants to pray the lines in the language they choose. Pray together "Ten Piedad de Nosotros/Have Mercy on Us."

For evening prayer, light a candle and incense. Begin with an opening prayer, hymn, and psalm. The reading will take place during the session (see the Resource Sheet "Liturgy of the Hours"). Extinguish the candle.

INTRODUCING THE SEASON

Introduce the season using the Handout "Paschal Mystery Background Information."

Great Temptations Distribute index cards and pens. Ask the members to write one of the greatest temptations a person could face. Have them find others who wrote similar temptations and form small groups. Post a sheet of newsprint, and have a marker handy. Ask each group to write their category on the newsprint (such as **TEMPTATIONS REGARDING MONEY, BREAKING A DIET, CONTROL OVER OTHERS**). Briefly read the categories aloud.

> **Facing temptation is one aspect of being human. Jesus faced his temptations while praying in the desert. In this session we will examine those temptations as we prepare to help others journey deeper into the paschal mystery during Lent.**

SCRIPTURE AND THE LITURGICAL SEASON

Use copies of the Handout "Breaking Open Scripture ..." for the current liturgical year (A, B, or C) with one of the first three options below to help the ministers (catechists, lectors, preachers, and others) enter the experience of the word.

Year A: Tempting Break a freshly baked loaf of bread, and place it on a platter. Invite the members to smell the aroma as you pass the bread around, saying the following:

> **Smell the tempting aroma of freshly baked bread. Think about the taste of the bread and how much you would like to eat it. (*After everyone smells the bread, cover it and put it aside.*) We are often tempted to eat foods even when we are not really hungry. As you listen to the Gospel, imagine how strong the temptation must have been in the desert for Jesus to turn stones into bread and eat when he was truly famished.**

Proclaim Matthew 4:1–11. Distribute Bibles and copies of the Handout "Breaking Open Scripture Year A: Matthew 4:1–11." Form groups to work through the sheets and discuss the questions. For shared wisdom, each group reports on the last question to the larger group.

Year B: Guided Meditation Invite everyone to get comfortable. Dim the lights and play reflective music. Invite them to close their eyes. Softly but loud enough for everyone to hear, read the Handout "Breaking Open Scripture Year B: Mark 1:12–15."

> **When you are ready, open your eyes and return to this space. Turn to one or two others and share images that are in your thoughts. (*Pause.*) Jesus gave a model for discernment. After baptism he felt driven to the desert. He needed to be alone with God. This aloneness was not a time of peace; it was a time of temptation and confusion. Jesus faced fears, hunger, and the possibility of death. Jesus overcame doubts and was ministered to by angels and fortified to do God's will.**

Form small groups. Give the leaders index cards with the following questions:

- **When have you had difficult times of discernment?**
- **What were/are your temptations or confusion?**
- **How do God's angels minister to you and lead you to do God's will?**

Year C: In the Desert Have the rocks, cactus, empty water bottle, and grocery bag handy. Use the Handout "Breaking Open Scripture Year C: Jesus in the Desert" as a guide to tell Luke 4:1–13. Distribute Bibles to three volunteers to look up the references for each of Jesus' answers: Deuteronomy 8:3, Deuteronomy 6:13, and Deuteronomy 6:16. Have them read the references. As a group, compare the Old Testament to Jesus' answers.

> **In Jesus' day people knew the Scriptures by heart. In our story Jesus and the tempter quoted Scriptures to each other. The tempter used the Scriptures to try to trick Jesus, but Jesus remained faithful to God.**

Desert Experience Discuss the following together or in small groups:

- **Why do you think the Spirit led Jesus into the desert?**
- **Describe how Jesus probably felt after praying and fasting for forty days.**
- **What are some things that tempted Jesus?**
- **What kinds of things tempt us today?**
- **What are some positive things the Spirit led you to do?**

Metanoia and the Church

> **Lent is the season of *metanoia,* a season of conversion. As individuals during Lent we are all on a *metanoia* path that leads us deeper into the paschal mystery. The church as a whole serves as a model of the conversion process. As church, we need to be ever more attentive to the needs of those who suffer.**

Distribute copies of the Handout "Conversion: A Church Task." Form small groups to suggest examples for each of the tasks. (*Option:* Offer copies of *Dogmatic Constitution on the Church* as a reference.) Each group reports on one idea for one item, repeating as needed.

Break Offer the snacks and beverages prepared by families who participate in faith formation programs.

APPLICATION

When ministers work together to prepare for the season, we grow through the sharing of ideas and build community among the ministerial team and faith community leaders. Choose one or more of the following options.

Scripture Faith Sharing Lectors, deacons, priests, catechists, and other ministers meet together or in small groups, look through lectionaries or proclaimer workbooks, and choose from readings for the season. They might use the Handout "Scripture Sharing Sheet" from the "Beginnings and Endings" session as a guide to develop and share insights. Discuss the following:

- **How do these readings lead us deeper into the paschal mystery?**

Lenten and Easter Symbols Have violet, red, and white cloths on a table or other surface. Among the cloths, display seasonal items, such as budding branches, desert plants, sand in a container, nails, crown of thorns, pretzels, bread, wine, ashes in a container, stones, a plain cross, Passion cross, a resurrection cross, spring flowers (Easter lilies, if available), an Easter egg, floating candle arrangements, and Easter breads. Invite each participant to come forward, pick up an item, and say how that symbol engages us in paschal mystery. Then discuss ways to incorporate the ideas into sessions, homilies, and other ministries.

Palm Cross Instructions Distribute copies of the Handout "Palm Cross Instructions," rulers, scissors, and construction paper to make crosses. Plan how to share the crosses with people who cannot come to Passion Sunday liturgy.

Temptations in the Mall Brainstorm how temptations confront various age groups at shopping malls. Form groups of three or four. Have each group choose one age group to represent and create a skit that takes place in a mall, showing how people of various ages might deal with temptations. Distribute scratch paper to jot down ideas, and offer props. (*Option:* Address temptations in magazine articles and advertisements, movies, and songs.)

Mission Support During Lent Catholics traditionally give extra support to missions. Distribute copies of the Handout "Mission Support," and have the participants learn about the work of some Catholic missionary groups. If possible, provide internet access from portable computers or in an office space to find information. Have the members log on to the suggested or similar sites, print information, and plan how to use this information in sessions, gatherings, and homilies. Choose one effort, such as Operation Rice Bowl of Catholic Relief Services, to encourage a Lenten giving project for the whole faith community.

The Scrutinies Distribute copies of the Handout "The Scrutinies." Go over the rituals together, and ask the participants to notice the similarities. Ask how each scrutiny can help the faith community become stronger while nurturing those joining the parish. In small groups ask them to suggest changes we could make in the church locally or globally so more people might receive living water, see the truth, and have abundant life.

The Stations for Today Have the participants gather in an outdoor area set up for the stations or in the church. Distribute copies of the Handout "Stations for Today," and pray the stations together. Ask the participants to retain the sheets to use during Lent.

Reconciliation Service Distribute copies of the Handout "Community Reconciliation Service." Designate who will do what, and plan a date, time, and location. Develop promotional materials such as bulletin announcements and posters. Decide if individual confession will be offered; if so, assign someone to invite priests and set up screened areas.

Seasonal Music Sing-Along Introduce the music minister(s). Distribute songbooks. Have the group practice singing music from liturgy for the upcoming liturgical seasons. Encourage the ministers to use some of this music in their gatherings to prepare participants for worship. (*Option:* Plan times for a music minister to visit the sessions to practice with the participants.) Decide how various groups will participate in events of the Triduum. Make the arrangements for the date, space, refreshments, publicity, and musicians.

LAUNCHING THE SEASON

- If necessary, distribute copies of the parish policies, and review together. Answer questions (noting any questions the parish staff or pastor need to clarify, and get back to the people with questions as soon as possible). Review policies as needed, including those for using the copier or requesting copies and arranging for a substitute.
- Distribute copies of the upcoming faith community calendar, and together consider future parish events. Determine what cooperation is needed regarding use of space and the timing of events.
- Ask if anyone feels the need for additional help, and make appointments to meet with those members soon. Ask if anyone needs a copy of the Resource Sheet "Ongoing Evaluation Form," and suggest that they make copies and use the form to evaluate their own ministries periodically.
- Give the date for the ministry formation session "Pentecost People."

MISSIONING

Gather in the prayer space. Have everyone stand in a circle.

Anointing with Oil

A woman poured oil on Jesus, foreshadowing his burial. Special oils are used in the sacraments of baptism, confirmation, anointing the sick, and holy orders.

Invite everyone to be anointed. Dip your thumb into fragrant oil, and make a cross on the forehead of the person on your left while saying, "You are anointed with the love of Christ. Go and spread the good news." Have that person turn, dip a thumb in the oil, and anoint the next person on the left while repeating the message. The final person anoints the leader.

We are all anointed in Christ in baptism. Let us pray as we more deeply enter into the paschal mystery. Please hold hands and repeat the following phrases:

Give us this day our daily bread;
and forgive us our trespasses as we forgive those who trespass against us;
and lead us not into temptation, but deliver us from evil.
In Jesus' name we pray. Amen.

Sing "Agnus Dei," in multiple languages, from *Breaking Bread* or Lenten music from liturgy

Closing Prayer Options For bilingual prayer, have everyone use copies of the Resource Sheet "Bilingual Prayers for Lent" to pray the lines of "Dios Justo y Misericordioso/God of Justice and Mercy" in their language of choice.

For evening prayer, close with the appropriate canticle, intercessions, and Our Father.

Pentecost People
April: Early Easter Season

FOCUS
To reflect together as ministers in this faith community about what it means to be Pentecost people.

Materials Needed

GENERAL PREPARATION

- Invite all ministers — lectors, catechists, potential substitutes, the Christian initiation team, environment committee, hospitality and outreach people, musicians, deacons, priests, and other adults — to attend this faith formation experience.
- Ask the ministers to make a **list of supply needs** for this season.
- Bring **nametags** and **pens.**
- Locate the Handouts in Appendix 1 for specific options in this session and the Resource Sheets in Appendix 2 for general use.
- If some members prefer to pray in Spanish, see "Prayer Options" below.

GATHERING

- Using the **Handout "'Welcome' in Various Languages"** in Appendix 1, fill in the blank section with a language common in your area. Make enough copies to have one section per participant. Cut apart and glue sections onto **index cards.**
- Prepare the prayer space with a **red or white and red cloth, floating candles in a clear container of water, a Bible** opened to a Gospel reading from Pentecost, and **fragrant oil in small open containers.** Bring a **percussion instrument** and **matches.** Ask a few ministers to act as anointers, and explain the prayer to them.
- *Prayer Options:* Consider using the bilingual prayers or copies of the **Resource Sheet "Liturgy of the Hours"** in Appendix 2 for Gathering and Missioning. Make copies of the **Resource Sheet "Bilingual Prayers for Pentecost"** in Appendix 2.

INTRODUCING THE SEASON

- Prepare a presentation about being Pentecost people using the ideas on the **Handout "Pentecost People Background Information"** in Appendix 1.

SCRIPTURE AND THE LITURGICAL SEASON

- *Year A: Gifts of the Spirit:* Ask two ministers to prepare to proclaim 1 Corinthians 12:3–13 and John 20:19–23. Make copies of the **Handout "Breaking Open Scripture Year A: Gifts of the Spirit"** in Appendix 1. Bring **Bibles.**
- *Year B: Fruits of the Spirit:* Ask two ministers to prepare to proclaim Galatians 5:22–25 and John 16:12–153. Make copies of the **Handout "Breaking Open Scripture Year B: Fruits of the Spirit"** in Appendix 1. Bring **Bibles.**
- *Year C: Names for the Holy Spirit:* Ask two ministers to prepare to proclaim Romans 8:8–17 and John 14:23–27. Make copies of the **Handout "Breaking Open Scripture Year C: Names for the Holy Spirit"** in Appendix 1. Bring **Bibles.**
- *Pentecost People:* Ask **1 minister of the word** to prepare to proclaim Acts of the Apostles 2:1–11.
- *Easter Symbols:* Make copies of the **Handout "Easter Symbols Mean Justice"** in Appendix 1. Bring symbolic items such as a **small hibachi with crumpled paper or other safe fire source, book about saints, water in a clear bowl, white clothing, scented oil, fresh bread,** and **wine in cup(s).**
- *Break:* Ask families who participate in faith formation programs to prepare and serve **snacks** and **beverages.**

Materials Needed

APPLICATION

Choose one or more of the following activities, varying the choices for each year of formation.

- *Scripture Faith Sharing:* Make copies of the **Handout "Scripture Sharing Sheet"** (from "Beginnings and Endings") in Appendix 1. Call to ask the participants to bring **lectionaries or proclaimer workbooks.**
- *Dramatic Enactments:* Make copies of the **Handout "An Enactment of Ezekiel 37:1–14"** in Appendix 1 (if needed for an example), or plan to have one group use the sheet. Call to ask the participants to bring **lectionaries or proclaimer workbooks.**
- *Pentecost Eggs:* See the **Handout "Pentecost Eggs"** in Appendix 1. Call several participants ahead of time to ask them to save and clean **whole eggshells.** Bring **egg coloring** (*optional*), **confetti, white glue,** and **pieces of color tissue paper.**
- *The Women's Stories:* Alternating years, make copies of the **Handout "Women of Faith Whom Jesus Knew"** or **"Spirit-filled Women of the Early Church"** in Appendix 1. Bring a **variety of art supplies, Bibles, pens, paper, costumes,** and **props.**
- *Celebration Noisemakers:* Make copies of the **Handout "Noisemakers"** in Appendix 1. Bring **various materials** for the participants to make several types of instruments.
- *Welcoming Neophytes:* With leaders of the initiation team (catechumenate program), plan for neophytes to attend the session.
- *Scripture Search:* Make copies of the **Handout "The Spirit in Scripture"** in Appendix 1. Bring **Bibles.**
- *Pentecost Celebration Planning:* Consult with the parish office about planning a whole-community celebration of Pentecost.
- *Seasonal Music Sing-Along:* Invite **1 or more music ministers** to sing and/or play a **musical instrument,** preparing songs that will be part of liturgy during this season. Bring **songbooks.** (*Option:* Ask if the music ministers are willing to visit the faith formation sessions to practice with children and other participants.)

LAUNCHING THE SEASON

- Review and prepare to distribute copies of a **list of parish policies,** including policies on record-keeping and tracking attendance, use of restrooms, shared space, arrival and departure expectations, keys, meeting for prayer before sessions, cleanup policies, noise levels, reimbursement procedures (if any), the pastor's expectations, office use, and how to obtain copies and materials.
- Make copies of the **faith community calendar.** Prepare to discuss activities that impact faith formation programs, including Pentecost and any summer recesses. Plan to recruit for summer or fall sessions, if necessary.
- Make copies of the **Resource Sheet "Ongoing Evaluation"** in Appendix 2.
- Plan the date to begin another year of ministry formation during the summer.

MISSIONING

- Bring **symbolic items** according to the **Handout "Easter Symbols Mean Justice"** in Appendix 1.

MUSIC

- Bring a **CD/tape player** and *Breaking Bread* songbooks or music from liturgy.
- Invite a **music minister** to lead the singing or play a **musical instrument.**

GATHERING

Welcome the ministers by name and offer nametags.

Mixer: Multilingual Welcome Distribute language cards prepared from the Handout "'Welcome' in Various Languages," one card for each participant. Ask them to circulate and greet one another using the expressions on the cards. The person greeted tries to guess the language.

Gathering Prayer After a few minutes, call the ministers to prayer by striking the percussion instrument. Light the candles. Mention that the disciples could speak words that welcomed others to the faith in many languages. Ask the group to call out the greeting after you state each language. Call out one language at a time, and encourage the ministers to respond.

> **Jesus, you gather us, your people, together from all parts of the world: Africa, Asia, South America, Europe, and North America. We disciples are a diverse group. We express our faith though hundreds of languages and many rich rituals. Divine Spirit, live in our midst, creating compassionate understanding and peace.**

The anointers pick up the containers with fragrant oil.

> **Oil is an ancient symbol for expressing the transfer of God's Spirit. As oil penetrates the body, the Spirit penetrates the receiver.**

Everyone holds out their palms. Going around the circle, the anointers anoint each person, saying the following:

> **Receive the power of the Holy Spirit.**

Conclude as follows:

> **Holy Spirit, come inspire us.**
> **Bring us courage to proclaim the good news through action and speech.**
> **Amen.**

Sing "Come, O Holy Spirit" or "Veni Sancte Spiritus" from *Breaking Bread* or a song about the Spirit from liturgy

Prayer Options For bilingual prayer, distribute copies of the Resource Sheet "Bilingual Prayers for Pentecost." Ask the participants to pray the lines in the language they choose.

For evening prayer, light a candle and incense. Begin with an opening prayer, hymn, and psalm. The reading will take place during the session (see the Resource Sheet "Liturgy of the Hours").

Extinguish any candles.

INTRODUCING THE SEASON

Give scriptural and liturgical information about being Pentecost people using the ideas on the Handout "Pentecost People Background Information."

SCRIPTURE AND THE LITURGICAL SEASON

Use copies of the Handout "Breaking Open Scripture …" for the current liturgical year (A, B, or C) with one of the first three options below to help the ministers (catechists, lectors, preachers, and others) to break open Scriptures for Pentecost.

Year A: Gifts of the Spirit Have the two ministers proclaim 1 Corinthians 12:3–13 and John 20:19–23. Assign small groups. Distribute the Handout "Breaking Open Scripture Year A: Gifts of the Spirit." Invite each group to discuss and then report what the members decide regarding one of the gifts.

Year B: Fruits of the Spirit Have the two ministers proclaim Galatians 5:22–25 and John 16:12–15. Assign small groups. Distribute the Handout "Breaking Open Scripture Year B: Fruits of the Spirit." Invite each group to discuss and then report what the members decide regarding the fruits ripening in this community.

Year C: Names for the Holy Spirit Have the two ministers proclaim Romans 8:8–17 and John 14:23–27. Assign small groups. Distribute the Handout "Breaking Open Scripture Year C: Names for the Holy Spirit." Invite each group to discuss and then report one name for the Holy Spirit and what it tells about how the Spirit works among us.

Pentecost People Invite the prepared reader to proclaim Acts of the Apostles 2:1–11.

> **The beginning of chapter 2 in Acts of the Apostles is one story that expresses the church's birth event.**
>
> • **What happened on that fateful, faith-filled day?**

While someone writes on newsprint, the group identifies the events. Together summarize points such as the following:

- The power of the Spirit came when followers gathered.
- An incredible noise entered the house.
- Something bright and fiery was seen, parted, and came to rest on each person.
- The noise attracted a large crowd of people who spoke a variety of languages.
- When the Galileans spoke of the mighty acts of God, everyone heard their own languages and understood.

Continue with the following:

> **The Book of Acts and the epistles preserved in the Bible tell how the church grew, what the early Christians believed, and how they acted.**

Easter Symbols The symbols of the Easter Vigil tell us who we are as people continuing Jesus' mission. Form at least nine pairs or small groups. Assign one Easter symbol from the Handout "Easter Symbols Mean Justice," repeating as needed. Invite the participants to experience the symbolic items.

> **Each small group will reflect on its symbol by using it in some way. Light the fire; read a Bible story; learn about names, and so forth. See the Handout for ideas. Prepare a prayer or other exercise to engage the group in the symbol in a way that calls us to justice.**

Plan to have sharing as the Missioning prayer.

Break Offer the snacks and beverages prepared by families who participate in faith formation programs.

APPLICATION

When ministers work together to prepare for the season, we grow through the sharing of ideas and build community among the ministerial team and faith community leaders. Choose one or more of the following options.

Scripture Faith Sharing Lectors, deacons, priests, catechists, and other ministers meet together or in small groups, look through lectionaries or proclaimer workbooks, and choose from readings for the season. They might use the Handout "Scripture Sharing Sheet" from the "Beginnings and Endings" session as a guide to develop and share insights.

Dramatic Enactments

The lectionary offers choices for readings during the Pentecost Vigil that are particularly rich and formative for Pentecost people.

In groups of eight, look over the readings for the Pentecost Vigil using lectionaries or proclaimer workbooks. Each group chooses one reading and creates a dramatic interpretation of the reading (see the Handout "An Enactment of Ezekiel 37:1–14" for an example). After the presentations, discuss the action of the Spirit in each reading.

Pentecost Eggs See the Handout "Pentecost Eggs" for complete instructions. Use the prepared eggshells. (*Option:* Color and dry the shells for ten minutes.) Have the participants stuff the eggshells with confetti until they are almost full. Use white glue to attach a small piece of color tissue paper over the opening and let it dry. On Pentecost break the eggs over one another's heads while acclaiming the gift of the Holy Spirit.

The Women's Stories Say something similar to the following:

The Sunday lectionary readings often omit stories about women. The sections that include women's stories sometimes occur in optional verses that may be omitted. In ministry we can expand on the lectionary readings to include the stories of women.

Distribute copies of the Handout "Women of Faith Whom Jesus Knew" or the Resource Sheet "Spirit-filled Women of the Early Church" (possibly alternating each year). Form small groups, assigning one woman to each group. Distribute Bibles, pens, paper, and art supplies. The groups read the information on the sheet about women in the Bible and create something to share that will tell the others about these women. It might be a poem, drawing, skit, song, or sculpture. After giving them time to make creations, each group shares with the larger group.

Celebration Noisemakers Discuss how the Spirit's coming was accompanied by a great amount of noise. Decide who in the faith community might enjoy noisemakers to celebrate Pentecost (such as those in the nursery or young children's groups, those in a care home, or those participating in a whole-community celebration). Distribute copies of the Handout "Noisemakers," and use the assorted materials to make noisemakers. Some of the ministers can deliver them to group leaders or care homes.

Welcoming Neophytes Connect the ministers with the neophytes who joined the baptized at the Easter Vigil and who are now beginning the experience of mystagogy. With leaders of the initiation team (catechumenate program), decide how to build community between the new members of the community and the catechetical groups and ministries. How will you invite and welcome new members into groups and ministries?

Scripture Search To small groups, distribute Bibles and copies of the Handout "The Spirit in Scripture." Look up the passages, and write down scriptural messages about the Spirit. For shared wisdom, each group shares the message of one passage with the larger group.

Pentecost Celebration Planning Make plans for a whole-community celebration of Pentecost. Assign people responsibilities for invitations and announcements, music, chairs, snacks and beverages, and activities. (*Option:* Plan to have a ministry fair with tables to inform and inspire members of various ages and abilities to become involved in ministry.) The group plans to lead on Pentecost day.

Seasonal Music Sing-Along Introduce the music minister(s) who will lead. Distribute songbooks. Have the group practice singing music from liturgy for the upcoming liturgical seasons. Encourage the ministers to use some of this music in their gatherings to prepare participants for worship. (*Option:* Plan times for a music minister to visit the sessions to practice with the participants.) As a group, decide if all the groups will meet for a whole-community Pentecost celebration or for any summer gatherings. If so, make the arrangements for the date, space, refreshments, publicity, and musicians.

LAUNCHING THE SEASON

- If necessary, distribute copies of the list of parish policies, and review the policies together. Ask for and answer questions (making a note of any questions the parish staff or pastor need to clarify, and get back to the people with questions as soon as possible). Review policies as needed, including those for using the copier or requesting copies and arranging for a substitute.
- Distribute copies of the upcoming faith community calendar, and together consider future parish events. Determine what cooperation is needed regarding use of space and the timing of events.
- Ask if anyone feels the need for additional help, and make appointments to meet with those members soon. Ask if anyone needs a copy of the Resource Sheet "Ongoing Evaluation Form," and suggest that they make copies and use the form to evaluate their own ministries periodically.
- Give the date for the ministry formation session for fall to begin another year.

MISSIONING

Gather in the prayer space with an assortment of symbols. Have selected groups lead the prayer by engaging the group in a symbol using their plans from this session. Conclude by asking the participants to respond, "Alleluia; alleluia."

> **Alleluia; alleluia. (*Response*)**
> **Come, Holy Spirit, fill the hearts of your faithful,**
> **and enkindle in them the fire of your love. (*Response*)**

Sing "O God, You Flamed On Sinai's Height," selected verses, or "Vayan Al Mundo/Go Out To The World" from *Breaking Bread* or a Pentecost song from liturgy

Closing Prayer Options For bilingual prayer, use the "Resource Sheet "Bilingual Prayers for Pentecost." Ask the participants to pray the lines in the language they choose.

For evening prayer, close with the appropriate canticle, intercessions, and Our Father.

Appendix 1

Formation Session Handouts

Breaking Open Scripture Year A: Matthew 16:21–27

Age-Appropriate Dramatizations

Jesus and Peter: A Drama

Invite those who will play Jesus, Peter, and the Biblical Person to put on costumes and stand aside. Say the following to the group:

Sit comfortably and close your eyes. Imagine that you are walking across a dry land under the hot sun.

Slowly turn the shoebox of sand end over end to evoke the sound of swirling sand. Tell about desert sights and sounds. Have the members open their eyes and describe what they imagined. Invite the three characters to present "Jesus and Peter: A Drama."

Biblical Person: (*beckons to Jesus and Peter to come nearer*) Folks, where are you headed? It is a hot time of day to be traveling.
Jesus: We are on our way to Jerusalem.
Biblical Person: Why are you going to Jerusalem?
Jesus: I was just telling my disciples that danger is waiting for me there. I will be killed, but I will be raised on the third day.
Peter: Jesus, do not even think such things! That must never happen to you.
Jesus: Get away from me, Peter. You have your mind on human things. I am about things of God.
Peter turns away.
Jesus: (*turns to the audience*) If you want to follow me, you will have to take up my cross too. If you lose your life for my sake, you will find your life. Some of you will be willing to do that.

The characters sit down. Lead the following discussion:

- What makes these words important today?

Talk about Peter's confusion, that the disciples expected a political kingdom to replace Roman rule, and that later the resurrection gave the disciples understanding.

- Why do you think Peter tried to stop Jesus?
- Why did Jesus argue with Peter?

Open the sandbox. Invite four members to dig in the sand and remove one scroll each. Have them read the scrolls. Discuss the community Jesus formed.

- What do you think these words tell us about living with Jesus in community?
- What do you think Jesus wanted to teach the disciples in this story?

Facial Expression Story

Before telling the story, ask the group, "What does your face look like when you are happy? surprised? afraid?" During the story make the appropriate faces, and invite the group to respond with the appropriate facial expressions.

Jesus was a teacher, but he did not teach about letters or numbers. Jesus taught about God's love. Jesus was **happy** he could teach people about God. He taught people to help one another, to share, and to work together. Jesus had a group of friends who helped him. They were **happy,** too, because they could help Jesus.

One day Jesus talked to his friends. "I must go to another city, a city called Jerusalem," he said. All of his friends were **surprised.** Why are you going there?" they asked. "It could be dangerous."

"Why are you so **surprised?**" Jesus asked them. "God wants me to go to Jerusalem, so I must go."

His friend Peter was **afraid.** Jerusalem was a big city. A lot of people were there. Peter did not know what would happen in Jerusalem. He did not want Jesus to go. "Do not go to Jerusalem, Jesus!" Peter cried. "I am **afraid.** I do not want you to go. Please stay here with your friends."

Jesus looked at his friends. He was **happy** to be with them. He thought about everything he taught them. He thought about God and how much God loved him. That made him very **happy.** Jesus was not **afraid.** He knew God would help him. Jesus said, "Do not be **afraid,** Peter. I must go. God wants me to go." Then Jesus gently put his hand on Peter's shoulder and said, "You are my friend, Peter, my disciple. Follow me."

Peter looked at Jesus. He knew Jesus cared for him. He would always follow him. Oh, how **happy** he was to share in God's love!

Breaking Open Scripture Year B: Mark 7:24–37

Explain that the lectionary reading takes place in the context of a larger story. To help make the meaning clear, the group will experience the whole story. Show the hand sign for "hear" by cupping your hand behind your ear. Ask the participants to make that hand sign each time they hear the word "hear" in the story. Have six or more participants act out the drama in the following parts: Narrator, Woman, Jesus, Crowd, and a man without a speaking part.

Drama: Jesus Listens and Heals

Narrator: Jesus traveled to a place called Tyre. He did not want anyone to *hear* he was there. Somehow a woman who had a sick daughter did *hear* that Jesus was nearby. She wanted Jesus to *hear* her.

Woman: Jesus, my daughter is very sick. I know you are the one who can heal her. Will you help us?

Jesus: Woman, you are not like us. Do you *hear* me? You come from a different country. I need to help my own people. They are first, not people such as you.

Woman: Please, Jesus. I know you are the one who can heal my daughter!

Jesus: Woman, now *hear* me. You understand God's ways. Go home. When you get there, your daughter will be healed.

Narrator: When the woman arrived home, she could *hear* her daughter laughing. Her daughter was well again. Through her faith Jesus worked a miracle. (*Pause.*) Jesus continued to travel. A little later the people brought Jesus a man who could not *hear* and had trouble speaking.

Crowd: (*brings man to Jesus*) Jesus, this man cannot *hear* or speak. You are the one who can help him.

Narrator: Jesus had learned from the woman to listen to everyone in need.

Crowd: Please, Jesus. This man needs your help.

Narrator: Jesus took him away from the people. (*Dramatize while saying the following:*) He put his fingers in the deaf man's ears and rubbed spit on his tongue.

Jesus: (*looks up to heaven and groans*) *Ephphatha!* Be opened!

Narrator: Then the man could *hear* and speak clearly! This was another special miracle!

Crowd: Thank you, Jesus, for helping our friend. We want everyone to *hear* about what you did.

Jesus: Please do not tell other people about this.

Narrator: Jesus was very humble, but he could not silence them.

Crowd: (*loudly*) Jesus does everything well! Jesus does everything well! He healed the sick and made the deaf *hear*. Jesus does everything well.

The performers sit.

Talking about the Gospel

In Jesus' time, to be deaf and mute meant more than just having a difficult time communicating and coping. Physical illnesses were considered spiritual illnesses, as if something were fundamentally wrong with people, therefore disconnecting them from God. As a result, such people were disconnected from family and the community. If you were deaf or mute during Jesus' time, no one would look at you or touch you. If someone took the risk of caring for you, they would likely suffer the same social fate.

Just as Jesus had to listen well to the woman with the sick daughter, we must also listen well to hear what God calls us to do. Just as Jesus had to listen well to the friends of the deaf man, we must also listen well to hear what God calls us to do.

Form small groups of members who minister with various age groups.

Discussion Questions: Mark 7:24–31

1. What type of person challenged Jesus, and what was the result?
2. When did Jesus shift his thinking?
3. How did listening change him?
4. What could Jesus do after opening himself to new possibilities?
5. How might the healed man's life change?
6. Why do you think Jesus told the crowd not to tell anyone about what happened?
7. How might we have closed ears to what God may be telling us?
8. What kind of spiritual healing do we need in our world today?
9. What are some things we can do to help bring such healing?

Breaking Open Scripture Year C: Luke 15–17

Distribute Bibles. Review the following parables of Luke 15–16:

> The Lost Sheep
> The Lost Coin
> The Lost Son
> The Rich Man and Lazarus

Discussion Questions

■ Imagine that you are disciples hearing these stories for the first time. What might you be thinking and feeling about what Jesus taught?

■ What conclusions might you draw about how Jesus expected you to live?

■ What did Jesus indicate about living simply and showing forgiveness to those who wrong us?

Turn to Luke 17:5–6. Have a volunteer read the verses aloud.

■ Keeping in mind the messages you just read in chapters 15 and 16, why do you think the disciples asked Jesus to increase their faith?

■ What challenges do you face trying to live out your beliefs and values?

■ What was Jesus' response to the disciples request?

Show the mustard seeds.

■ Imagine the deep roots of a mulberry tree. How do you think people reacted when Jesus told the story about the small seed of faith commanding a mulberry tree to uproot itself and replant in the sea?

■ What do you think Jesus was trying to say?

■ Can you think of any examples of people whose simple actions have made a big difference?

Have a volunteer read Luke 17:7–10.

■ What was Jesus saying to us?

■ What difference do you think you make as you live out your faith in your day-to-day life?

Faith and Ordinary Time

"Whoever is faithful in a very little is faithful also in much" (Lk 16:10).

This saying of Jesus points to one of the most profound and life-transforming truths it is possible to know — that is, the sacredness of the ordinary. How we live in our daily lives actually does matter! This week most of us will not be part of world-shaping events, but we may have a chance to give someone a cup of water, offer encouragement, visit a shut-in, lead a faith formation session, share a meal, tell a child a story, go to choir practice, or feed a neighbor's pet. The realm of God is powerfully present in the ordinary day-to-day details of our lives and of the world in which we live.

Imagine huge vertical towers juxtaposed with rolling green fields; modern communication lines radiating out from seemingly impassable concrete walls; a gravity-defying steel bridge arching across space; and then, seemingly out of nowhere, a luxuriant green vine wrapping intimately around the whole scene. We remember that God's dynamic, life-giving presence is active in the tumult of a modern city as much as in the calm of a rural landscape: in our own day as much as in Jesus' time.

The word "ordinary" refers to that which is established, regular, and placed in the order of our daily activity. Something is ordinary when it is usual and apt to come around in the regular common order of succession of events. Synonyms for "ordinary" are "common," "customary," "usual," "undistinguished," or even "of little note." When we pay attention to ordinary things, we immediately lift them out of the ordinary, and they become icons of the holy.

Jesus demanded that the disciples make some hard choices about their loyalties to be followers. Jesus feasted with tax collectors and sinners to the chagrin of the religious authorities. Jesus was clear about a preference for the marginalized. Throughout Ordinary Time we enter the struggle of disciples learning to think beyond the ordinary conventional wisdom of their day about such things as wealth, social privilege, whom to invite to dinner, and the treatment of those who are oppressed, overlooked, suffering, and outcast in society. Jesus is the master at turning people's attention toward ordinary things that people tend to take for granted and then helping us to look in such a way that we can never see them the same way again. It is no wonder that Jesus became such a threat to people in authority. While they put all their efforts into upholding the social and religious conventions of their day, Jesus' every word and action called these very things into question. Simple daily activities such as sharing a meal became powerful vehicles for the emergence of God's new realm of justice and mercy.

We live out our faith in the context of time. The ordinary things we do every day reflect our relationship with the holy. We can make a difference in the world here and now. A lived, everyday faith mirrors Christ for the world. Everyday faith offers hope in the midst of all the ordinary struggles of ordinary people.

Ministers are in a unique and very special position. As role models and faith-filled individuals, we are entrusted to nurture the developing faith of the children, youth, and adults in our faith community. The liturgical cycle helps us to pray what we experience in the cycle of life.

Faith Is ...

Faith is sometimes like confidence or trust:

trust in ourselves, in our world, and in God.

- Rachael, age four, was walking past her new daycare for the first time. She saw all the kids playing on the playground and burst out, "Oh, look! There are all my new friends."

Faith is sometimes like commitment or doing what we believe.

- While Mr. K was in the hospital, the faith community youth group kept his grass cut and cleaned his house. When he came home, he found food in the fridge and a friendly "Welcome Home" note on the table. He wanted to pay the youth group for what they did. "No," they said, "we are just doing what we are supposed to do as Christians."

- Every year the Social Action Committee holds a "toxic waste day." They collect household garbage that damages the environment (such as paint, solvents, or batteries) and take it to a special toxic waste site. Their sign announcing the day says "Faith in action — caring for God's earth."

Faith is sometimes like feeling God close to us.

- Mrs. B had a serious heart attack. The doctors wanted to do an operation but they were not sure it would help. Mrs. B might die during the operation. Mrs. B said to her friend, "I am a little afraid, but deep inside I feel very safe and peaceful. I know God is with me; whatever happens, I will be fine."

- Kristy had a dream one night. She shared that dream with a close friend. "I dreamed God was calling me, asking me to do something very important. When I woke up, I was sure that God was with me, asking me to do whatever God wants me to do."

What is faith like for you?

Scripture Sharing Sheet

Catechists, lectors, homilists, and all ministers need to experience

an ongoing conversation with the Scriptures to prepare for ministry and deepen faith.

They need to meet regularly to break open the texts with others.

Preparation for Weekly Meetings

1. Read a text aloud. Write down words and images that stand out. Note any initial impressions. Maintain an open mind. Be aware that every biblical text has many levels.

2. Consult commentaries. Write down new insights. Note any disagreement among scholars.

3. Plan a gathering with other ministers, and decide who will present the text. Use a variety of ways to present and explore Scripture.

Meeting with Other Ministers

A. Proclaim and explore the word.

1. One or more members proclaim or creatively present the text.
2. Share first impressions.
3. Share insights from scholarly research.

B. Discuss those who hear the word through your presentation as a catechist, lector, or homilist.

1. How do these texts speak to their needs?
2. What factors in your local situation influence how the hearers will respond?

C. Let all voices in the group be heard.

1. What confrontations are stimulated by these Scripture messages?
2. What are the possible different points of view?
3. How might hearing these Scripture messages in new ways inspire someone to change?
4. What do we risk in responding to this text?

D. Reflect on the work these passages inspire the church to do.

1. What can we accomplish together?
2. How does this text criticize the church today?

E. Prepare for ministry.

1. Catechists consider their session outlines, their participants, and the liturgical year. Share possible ways to present this text.
2. Lectors practice pronouncing difficult words, intonation, and emphasis. Get critical feedback and adjust proclamation styles.
3. Homilists receive input and plan points pertinent for the local community.
4. Other ministers discuss how the Scripture relates to their ministries. What call to action or change does it indicate?

Plan the date, time, and place for the next faith sharing gathering.

Enabling Faith-in-Action

Incarnational faith transforms our life. Christ calls us to live out our faith in the world and put our beliefs into practice. We are called to participate together in the creating of God's Shalom. Faithful actions do not always need to be big ones; God multiplies even our smallest contributions.

The call to justice on behalf of the oppressed is not optional. It must be an integrated part of out faith. The prophet Amos proclaimed for God, "I hate, I despise your festivals .... Even though you offer me your burnt offerings and grain offerings, I will not accept them .... But let justice roll down like waters, and righteousness like an ever-flowing stream" (Amos 5:21,22,24).

Jesus described the entrance into God's realm in a parable of sheep and goats. Those who were excluded or outside were those who failed to feed the hungry, clothe the naked, or visit those who were sick or in prison. When we fail to show love and care for the world around us, we fail God.

The following are some tips for working on outreach or faith-in-action:

- Form a group and combine fun with caring.

- Choose concrete and tangible projects that all the members can accept. Do not coerce anyone to agree with any particular cause.

- Connect action with faith by discussing the biblical story and Christian tradition.

- Do not "guilt trip" anyone. Respect individual differences.

- Affirm positive actions.

Household of Faith

People become Christians by accepting new beliefs. People who enter through this door often discover the Gospel through reading, the example of friends, Bible study, and discussion. They may have many questions about their own long-held beliefs and those they associate with the church.

People become Christians through experiences of God and Jesus that call them to new life. People who enter through this door often experience powerful "conversion" experiences.

People become Christians by being born into Christian families. They are nurtured in environments of Christlike living. People who enter through this door are members of families who worship on Sundays, join in faith community events, attend Catholic schools, and participate in faith formation programs.

People become Christians by doing works of justice and mercy. People who enter through this door express their concerns for others through action and prayer. They join with others who take steps to help the poor and marginalized.

Our faith journeys are personal and unique because we are unique. For each of us, the search for God is different from others' because we are different from everyone else. Because God is infinitely creative and visioned us as who we are, the Gospel promises many routes to God and to *the church*. Imagine a "household of faith" that has many different rooms, doors, and windows but is one household under God.

Faith Hand Signs

Sign language allows people to participate actively in faith formation using their whole bodies in the experience. It also helps build solidarity and communication with those who have hearing difficulties. We can use sign language in several ways, such as the following:

- Tell an entire story or special words in a story in sign language.

- Teach members several signs so they can participate throughout a story or prayer.

- Teach the main point in sign language.

- Use simple and common signs to tell a message without using voice.

To continue using hand signs with storytelling, check out a book from your local library. Sign language can add a new dimension to your storytelling by incorporating visual and bodily expression and beauty to your stories.

Advent *— Begin with both index fingers pointing up, with your hands in front of and higher than your head and your palms facing in. Bring both hands down while turning your palms down, ending with both index fingers pointing down in front of your chest.*

Alleluia *— Bring both your open hands, with the palms facing each other and fingertips pointing up, together in front of your chest. Raise both hands (in the "A" position) near each shoulder, moving them outward in small circles. Repeat the movement.*

Amen *— Close your left hand over your right closed hand, and move them slowly up toward your chest.*

Angel *— Touch the fingertips of both bent hands to your shoulders, with the palms facing down and elbows close at your sides. Turn the wrists outward, and bend the hands up and down.*

Bible *— Open both hands, with your palms facing. Place the tip of your left middle finger on your right palm and then your right middle tip on your left palm. (This is the sign for "Jesus.") Now place your palms together, with your thumbs up, and open as if you are opening a book.*

Christmas *— With your right hand in the "C" position, move the hand from near the left shoulder, with the palm down, in a large arc ending near your right shoulder, with the palm facing outward. This initialized sign follows the shape of a wreath.*

Disciple *— With both hands in the "D" position and your left hand in front of your right hand, with the palms facing forward, simultaneously move both hands forward in front of your body in double arcs.*

Easter *— Beginning with the palms of both hands facing each other in front of each shoulder, twist your wrists, and then repeat the movement. (You can also do this with one hand.)*

(more on next page)

God — *Move your right hand, with the palm facing left and fingertips pointing up and slightly forward, in an arc toward the forehead and down in front of your face.*

 Peace / Shalom — *Bring both open hands together, and reverse hands while holding the palms together; in a smooth movement from the front of your mouth, move downward and outward to about shoulder height at the lower chest level.*

Hello, New Friend

 Hello — *Wave your right hand, with the palm facing out.*

 **Pray** — *Place your palms together, with the fingertips slanted up, and rotate in a slight arc toward your body.*

 New — *Hold up both palms, and cross your right palm over the left palm, moving forward and up.*

 **Spirit** — *Holding your right hand in the "F" position and the left hand in the "O" position, with your right hand inside the left hand and close to the body, move your right hand upward in front of your chest.*

 Friend — *Interlock your right and left index fingers, with the right index over the left.*

 *Welcome*

Jesus Said, "Love One Another"

 Jesus — *Using both hands, touch the left middle finger to your right palm, and then touch the right middle finger to your left palm.*

 Said — *Hold your right index finger in front of your mouth, and roll it forward in a circular movement.*

 Love — *Cross your arms at the wrists across your chest, with the palms facing the body.*

 One Another — *Make a fist with each hand, with both thumbs sticking out and one thumb pointing up and one thumb pointing down. Move both hands in a counterclockwise motion while the thumb pointing down circles around the thumb pointing up.*

How Do I Know the Group Experience Is a Success?

Sometimes it is tempting to measure success by the number of times people agree with us or say things we want them to say. It can sometimes feel like surviving a session is success. The real signs of success relate to the purpose of the gathering, the trust built, and the faith and meaning that we discover. True success comes when we do not lock into "right" answers or expected actions.

As you perform the following "self-exam," think about what real success means to you. For each pair of statements, consider which one you truly most often use as a sign of success.

I consider the experience a success when ...

a. People raise questions that are important to them.
b. All the questions I ask are answered correctly.

a. We can disagree while still respecting one another's opinions.
b. No one disagrees with anyone else.

a. People feel a sense of pride in something the groups works on together.
b. The project gets completed.

a. We can discover new and different meanings in a story or a symbol.
b. The group learns what the symbol or story really means.

a. We laugh a lot with one another and have fun.
b. Everyone is quiet and submissive.

a. People openly discuss what is happening in their lives; they express real feelings, including anger and sadness.
b. We stay strictly on topic.

a. We solve a group problem together.
b. Everyone does what I direct.

a. People feel that their opinions count.
b. Everyone listens to what I tell them and respects my authority.

a. We change what I planned and discover something meaningful.
b. We stick to business and complete what I planned.

a. We run out of time because everyone is so interested and involved.
b. We get everything done.

If you have many "a" answers, things might get confusing at times, but you are probably leaving plenty of room for the creative movement of God's Spirit to enable everyone to grow in faith. If you find that most of your answers are "b," you might want to challenge yourself to be more open-ended and flexible with your group. Allow more flexibility in the process, and let the results surprise you.

Breaking Open Scripture Year A: Matthew 24:37–44 and Matthew 3:13–17

Christ's Coming

Read Matthew 24:37–44 for the First Sunday of Advent.

- How do you react to this as an Advent passage?

- For whom are we waiting?

- The passage sharply contrasts with secular attitudes that we experience during this season. How do you reconcile this reading with preparing to celebrate the joy of Jesus' birth?

Baptism

The Christmas season ends with the feast of Jesus' baptism, the beginning of his active ministry. Read Matthew 3:13–17.

- What does it mean to have God's favor rest on us?

- If you had not been baptized, would you be a different person today? How?

- What does this feast's position in the church year, so closely following Christmas and Epiphany, say to us?

Breaking Open Scripture Year B: Mark 13:33–37

Actively Watching Discussion Questions

- How does purposeful watching help us to perceive what we really should be doing?

- What kinds of things do we do while actively watching?

- What things should we expect for the reign of God to become complete?

- How can our expectations and actions bring about the completion of the reign of God?

Breaking Open Scripture Year C: When Jesus Comes Again

(for Luke 21:25–28)

Together proclaim the Scripture with movement.

When Jesus comes again, ... *Motion with your hands toward your chest.*

People will see signs in the sun, ... *Raise your hands up and to the left.*

In the moon, ... *Move your uplifted hands to the right.*

And in the stars. . . . . *Move your uplifted hands back and forth.*

The people will worry, ... *Put your hands on your cheeks.*

And they will wonder what is happening. . . . . *Scratch your head.*

People will be frightened, ... *Cross your hands across your heart.*

For the world will be dazed, ... *Put your hands over your head.*

And the power of the heavens will be shaken. . . . . . . *Kneel your with hands on your head.*

Then the people will see the Son of Man. . . . . *Put your hands down and raise your head.*

He will come in power and glory. . . . . *Raise your hands to the heavens.*

So when these signs begin to happen, stand up! . . . . . *Stand with your hands raised.*

Your salvation is near. . . . . *Applaud.*

Small-Group Sharing

- What are some entrapments that pull people away from God?

- What anxieties creep into our daily lives?

- How can we conquer these temptations and worries?

Seasons Merge

The Season of Advent

Advent begins the church year, with a mood of hope and expectation. "Advent" means "coming," and it is when Christians prepare to celebrate the coming of the Christ-child and anticipate the fulfillment of God's promises.

The Advent readings are rich with the messages of the prophets. They ask people to turn around and reform. The prophets were concerned with the gap between how people worshiped and how they lived their faith. They struggled with the problems of government and politics and of public morality and social justice. In these situations they saw aspects of God's character and purpose, judgment and mercy. They offered hope in the midst of crises.

The prophets increasingly came to look forward to a time when God's purpose would be fully revealed. The Gospel writers believed the coming of Jesus fulfilled this purpose. By understanding and reflecting on the prophets during Advent, we can better understand the setting into which Jesus was born and the prophetic tradition he inherited.

The liturgical color of Advent is violet, a color generally associated with Lent and penance, but the church no longer thinks of Advent as a "little Lent." Advent is not about Lenten-style penitence but about messianic expectation. The rose color of the Third Sunday of Advent reminds us of the joy that God became flesh and lived as one of us. Penance means "turning," and during Advent we turn and focus on God, who was born poor, humble, and homeless in a manger.

Advent may be the most difficult season of the liturgical year to keep as a season for its own wonderful sake since the world around us starts advertising Christmas before Halloween. Plan to explain that as Catholics, we have a different way to celebrate the weeks before Christmas. Our visual symbols, Advent wreaths and calendars and Jesse Trees, remind us why this is a season of preparation. We hold off singing carols until Christmas. Advent music conveys the mood of waiting and expectation. Put prayers into action and share God's love for the world about which we sing. Plan a parish Advent project that will bring joy to needy families on Christmas.

The Season of Christmas

Christmas, the shortest season of the church year, begins at sundown on Christmas Eve. It is a joyous celebration of arrival: Emmanuel, "God-with-us." Christmas season includes the feasts of the Holy Family; Mary, the Mother of God on January 1; Epiphany; and the Baptism of the Lord. The first week of Ordinary Time begins on the Monday after, so there is not a First Sunday in Ordinary Time.

The date for Christmas may have been taken from a Roman feast. According to one theory, the Roman church of the fourth century began to celebrate the Nativity of Christ on December 25 as a way of coopting the "birthday of the unconquered sun," celebrated on the same day. Others hold that Christian thinkers of the same period, who already associated Christ with the sun, paid particular attention to the solstices and equinoxes. Because Luke 1:26 places Jesus' conception six months after John the Baptist's, whose birthday we came to celebrate on the summer solstice, Christians naturally came to celebrate Jesus' nativity around the winter solstice. Whichever theory is correct, Christmas has always been associated with the return of daylight and the decrease of darkness. Christ is the light of the world, a belief suggested in the seasonal colors of white and gold.

The Incarnation Season

We might consider the combined seasons of Advent and Christmas as the incarnation season. This is the time of year when we remember that "the Word became flesh and lived among us" (Jn 1:14). We take four weeks to reflect on that unique and marvelous event in history that guarantees us everlasting life. We recall how the Jewish people waited for a Messiah for thousands of years and are still waiting. We prepare wonderful celebrations with friends, food, gifts, and music for Christmas. We look forward to that eventual time when there will be no more hunger and violence in the world.

Christ came incarnate as a helpless, homeless, voiceless baby, needy in every way. We are accordingly called to see the face of Jesus in needy people and to speak on behalf of those who have no voice or power in our world. We are called to live as one, following the One who was most humble, meek, and strong in the ways of God. The joys of the Christmas celebration are magnified when we spend the Advent season preparing and renewing our lives with Christ and seeking justice for the poor.

Incarnation Season

The Manger Means Justice

In the beginning was the Word, … and the Word was God …. And the Word became flesh" (Jn 1;1,14). Christ, out of love for humanity, individually and collectively, came to dwell as one among us. In choosing to become one with humanity, God Incarnate has dignified all human existence. Each person's dignity is affirmed by an indissoluble unity with Christ who was born one with us.

As incarnate Word, Christ became identified in a unique way with the human condition. The value of each person's dignity was raised by the presence of Christ in the manger and was sealed by the blood of Christ on the cross.

Jesus, an infant swaddled in the manger, had total dependency. God chose to be born a baby whose parents were on the road, a baby who had no voice to speak and express needs. At the moment of birth Christ was turned away, outcast by those who had a comfortable roof over their heads. Taking on human form as a baby, God identified with the most vulnerable of people, those who depend on others for their daily food, clothing, and shelter. With the manger as a bed, Jesus' first home was temporary. Having had no permanent place at the time, God Incarnate became a child born into a family in transition and, so, has identity with those in poor and needy circumstances.

God, born among us, found a manger for dwelling, not palatial surroundings. Thus, God has a special identity with the meek and elevated the dignity for those of humble birth. The meager circumstances of Jesus' birth give the most defenseless and needy of persons a special solidarity with Jesus. In church social teaching, this is called a preferential option for the poor.

Jesus of the manger cries out for justice for those whose cries are not heard. Following in Christ's footsteps, the church, then, is called to affirm dignity and seek justice for every human person. Seeing Christ in every person, followers seek justice for the meek, the dependent, the vulnerable, the poor, those in transition, and those without a voice for themselves.

Janet Miller, "The Manger Means Justice," *The Catechist's Connection* (December 2003). © Janet Miller.

Discussion Questions

1. How do the needs of the baby lying in the manger inspire you?

2. Considering that Jesus was born away from home, how does this inspire to help migrants and immigrants?

3. Because the Baby Jesus could not voice his needs, how can you use your voice to defend the helpless?

4. How do you strive for justice for those who are as vulnerable as the Baby Jesus was in the manger?

Jesse Tree

To make a Jesse Tree, secure a small branch in a can of plaster of paris.
Each day of December read the Scripture, design an ornament,
and add the ornament to the tree. Read the passage for Jesus on Christmas Eve.

Adam and Eve: *Genesis 3:1–24*

Noah and His Family: *Genesis 8:11–21;*
9:8–11

Abraham and Sarah: *Genesis 15:1–8;*
17:1–22

Isaac: *Genesis 17:17–19; 21:1–7*

Rebecca: *Genesis 22:1–18*

Jacob: *Genesis 28:10–22*

Leah: *Genesis 29:31–36*

Tamar: *Genesis 38:12–14*

Joseph: *Genesis 37:1–11; 45:6–20*

Miriam: *Exodus 2:1–4; 15:20–21*

Moses: *Exodus 14:10–31; 20:1–17*

Rahab and Salmon: *Joshua 2:1–14*

Ruth and Boaz: *Ruth 2:1–3; 4:7–12*

Jesse: *1 Samuel 16:11–13; Isaiah 11:1*

David and Bathsheba: *1 Samuel 16:17–23;*
2 Samuel 12:24–25

Solomon: *1 Kings 4:29–34; 8:14–24*

Judith: *Judith 8:4–17*

Esther and Mordecai: *Esther 2:7,16–18;*
14:18–19

Isaiah: *Isaiah 11:3–10*

Joseph: *Matthew 1:18–25*

Angel of the Annunciation: *Luke 1:26–38*

Mary: *Luke 1:46–55*

John the Baptist: *Luke 1:57–80*

Jesus: *Luke 2:1–7*

Advent Wreath

An Advent wreath traditionally has four candles (three violet and one rose/pink, or four white candles) arranged in a circle with greenery. Violet ribbon accents are sometimes added to the white candles. We light one candle for each week of Advent, lighting the rose candle on the Third Sunday of Advent. Flames remind us of the light of Christ in the world. The endless circle of evergreens remind us of everlasting life.

Option 1

Make a wreath using two 12-by-2-inch pieces of wood. Drill ½-inch holes into the four ends about 1 inch from the end of the wood. In the center of one piece, drill another ½-inch hole. Put the piece of wood with three holes on top of the other to make a cross shape and nail them together. Place one rose and three violet candles in the outer holes to form a ring and one white candle in the center. Decorate with fire-safe greenery.

Option 2

Bring five small glass jars, with one white, one rose, and three violet candles that fit inside the jars. Place the candleholders and candles on a circular tray, with the color candles on the outside and the white candle in the center. Arrange fire-safe greenery among the candles.

Option 3

Use self-hardening clay to form a ring, or use a purchased foam ring. Make four evenly spaced holes to hold candles. Insert one rose and three violet candles in the holes. Decorate with violet ribbon. For the Christmas season, you may place a Christ candle (white candle) in a holder in the center.

Magi Gifts

The feast of the Epiphany comes near the end of the incarnation season. We celebrate the feast every year, and it reminds us that Jesus came for all people, not just a chosen group of the faithful. We might interpret the significance of the gifts they brought in many ways.

Gold

Gold has certainly always been a precious commodity. It was the prized medium of exchange in civilizations throughout the world wherever it is found. Even today gold is an internationally traded commodity and the basis for many monetary systems.

Frankincense

Frankincense is considered the "holy anointing oil" in the Middle East. It is extracted from the gum (resin) of a plant that originated in Somalia. It has been used for healing purposes and in religious ceremonies for thousands of years. It was valued more than gold during ancient times and was possessed only by those with great wealth.

Frankincense has been used to treat a wide variety of physical and emotional conditions. Researchers today have discovered that frankincense is high in sesquiterpenes, which help stimulate the limbic system of the brain (the center of emotions) as well as the hypothalamus, pineal, and pituitary glands. Frankincense is now being researched and used therapeutically in European hospitals and is being investigated for its ability to improve human growth hormone production.

Myrrh

Myrrh has also been used for millennia for healing and anointing purposes. The Arabian people use it for chapped and cracked skin and wrinkles. It was used in biblical times for embalming. Like frankincense, it comes from a plant originating in Somalia and has high levels of sesquiterpenes, so it also affects emotions and hormones. It is widely used today in oral hygiene products.

1. What do the three gifts signify about Jesus to you?

2. What precious gifts would visitors today offer Jesus, and what would they signify?

3. What gifts do you offer Jesus for all that God does for you?

Breaking Open Scripture Year A: Matthew 4:1–11

Jesus relied on the word of God in Scripture to resist evil. Find Matthew 4:1–11 in a Bible. Discuss the three types of temptation Jesus faced using the following guide:

1. Jesus may have been tempted to use his incredible powers to turn the stones into bread. (*Find the applicable verses.*)

   a. What good could Jesus have accomplished for a hungry person by turning stones into bread?

   b. Why was this not an acceptable way for Jesus to use his powers?

2. Jesus may have been tempted to prove he was the Messiah by jumping from the parapet to see if angels would save him. (*Find the applicable verses.*)

   a. Why might it have seemed like a good thing for Jesus to be proven the Messiah?

   b. Why was this not an acceptable way for Jesus to use his powers?

3. Jesus may have considered the possibility of using his abilities to establish himself as a powerful earthly king. (*Find the applicable verses.*)

   a. What good could Jesus have accomplished as an earthly king?

   b. Why was this not an acceptable way for Jesus to use his powers?

For help in resisting these temptations, Jesus relied on messages from Scripture, the word of God. (*Find the verses where Jesus quotes Scripture.*)

On what Scriptures do you rely during times of temptation?

Breaking Open Scripture Year B: Mark 1:12–15

A Reflection Based on Mark 1:12–15

To include the background for the Gospel story, the reflection begins with Mark 1:9.

Invite the members to assume comfortable positions and close their eyes if they wish.

Take yourself back in time, back to the River Jordan. Imagine that you are Jesus, walking along a river. (*Pause.*) John is baptizing crowds of people. (*Pause.*) You walk up to John and say, "Baptize me too." John says a very curious thing, "You, Jesus, should baptize me." (*Pause.*) John finally agrees. You go down, down, down into the water. You hold your breath until you feel you may pass out. (*Pause.*) Desperate for air, you throw yourself up out of the water. Shaking the water from your face, you open your eyes and see the most amazing sight. The sky is filled with brilliant light. This light is pouring out on you, filling you to the depth of your being. (*Pause.*) No one else seems to be able to see it, but a voice from the light source talks to you and says, "You are my Son, the Beloved; with you I am well pleased." (*Pause.*)

In a daze you pull yourself up the bank of the river. The crowds are still pushing around John. No one notices that something most amazing has happened to you. What can this mean? (*Pause.*)

You stumble away, somewhat confused. You feel desperate to get away from this crowd. You need to go someplace alone to figure this out. You feel driven to the desert to pray. (*Pause.*) You stay in the wilderness for many days, sucking the juices from the small plants you find to stay alive. You meditate by day. What does God say to you? (*Pause.*) At night you see the eyes of wild beasts lurking in darkness. How do you feel? (*Pause.*)

Yes, you are scared. You think thoughts of rejecting what God wants you to do. (*Pause.*) In hunger and fear, you look death in the face. (*Pause.*) Your fears subside as you realize that God is with you. (*Pause.*) You vow to do God's will always, even in the face of fear and danger and death. (*Pause.*)

Angels suddenly come and minister to you. How do you feel now? (*Pause.*) You are rested and rejuvenated, ready for the task God showed you. With a new energy, you begin your trek out of the desert, away from solitude, and back to your home village. (*Pause.*) There you learn terrible news; John was arrested! John? How can this be? John, your beloved idol, your cousin and hero, is in prison! (*Pause.*) Who will carry on his work? (*Pause.*)

You accept the challenge. With courage, energy, and hope, you march into Galilee proclaiming God's good news: "The time of fulfillment is here! The reign of God is upon us. Repent. Believe the good news." (*Pause.*)

Invite the members to open their eyes slowly.

Breaking Open Scripture Year C: Jesus in the Desert

Place the rocks where the members can see them,

with the cactus plant in the center of the rocks.

Jesus was getting ready. He had been to the River Jordan, where he met John. John baptized Jesus by dunking him in the river. God sent the Holy Spirit to Jesus. Jesus knew it was time to get ready, time to get ready to do the work for which God sent him to the world.

Jesus went off into the desert to pray. The desert was a rocky place (*indicate the rocks*), with prickly plants (*indicate the cactus*), and it was very hot and dry. Jesus walked. Jesus prayed. Jesus slept. Then Jesus walked some more, prayed some more, and slept some more. Jesus did this for forty days. (*Flash your hands four times.*)

At the end of forty days, Jesus was so tired and was so thirsty (*bring out the empty water bottle*), but he had a hard time finding water to drink. Jesus was so hungry (*shake out the empty bag*), but he had a hard time finding food to eat.

Just then someone came to see Jesus. The Tempter came to see Jesus. The Tempter thought he could get to Jesus, thought he could turn Jesus away from God.

The first thing the Tempter said to Jesus was this: "If you are really the Son of God, take these rocks and turn them into bread." (*Indicate the rocks.*)

Jesus shook his head at the Tempter. (*Shake your head no.*) Jesus reminded the Tempter what the Bible says. Jesus said, "It says in the Bible that we are not to live by bread alone. We have to remember to live by God's words."

The second thing the Tempter said to Jesus was this: "Look at all the countries in the world. If you worship me, I will give them all to you."

Jesus shook his head at the Tempter. (*Shake your head no.*) He reminded the Tempter what the Bible says. Jesus said, "It says in the Bible that we are to worship only God. We have to remember to serve only God."

The third thing the Tempter said to Jesus was this: "We are up in a high place, but I want you to throw yourself down. It says in the Bible that the angels will take care of you."

Jesus shook his head at the Tempter. (*Shake your head no.*) He reminded the Tempter what the Bible says. Jesus said, "It says in the Bible that we are not to tempt God. We have to remember that God does not want us to trick one another."

The Tempter knew he had lost, so he went away. But Jesus knew the Tempter would be back. Jesus knew he would have to continue praying to God. Jesus knew he would have to continue relying on God.

Paschal Mystery Background Information

The journey begins again! Once again we are invited to renew our journeys that lead us deeper into the paschal mystery. From the first call to go into the desert, through the Passion and the resurrection, and to the driving Spirit pushing us onward, we are encouraged to grow in our faith during this Lent–Easter season.

Lent begins with the symbolic journey that Christians take with Jesus. The path of the paschal mystery leads toward Easter and eternal life. The season of Lent invites us into a more reflective mood. It is a deepening time. We stop, look, listen, and attend to the parts of our lives that we often neglect. We open ourselves in new ways to the transforming power of God's Spirit. This Lenten path is not easy, but those who go before us assure us that many blessings exist for those who set out on the journey.

We emerge from this path during the Triduum. We rejoice at Jesus' triumphal entry into Jerusalem only to suffer with Jesus during the events that led to the cross. On Easter we discover the empty tomb with the women and the other disciples. With Mary Magdalene, we recognize Jesus, who calls us by name. We are called to experience the resurrection not only with our minds but also with our hearts and our very beings. The journey we begin during Lent never ends. The Holy Spirit challenges us and guides us to continue our transformation in the joy and belief in the resurrection.

Liturgical Year

Lent begins the Easter or resurrection cycle of the church's liturgical calendar and calls us deeper into the paschal mystery. The season of Lent begins on the Sunday after Ash Wednesday, the day that reminds us of our need to die to our old selves to be raised to new life with Christ. The Triduum is the final commemoration of Christ's Passion, death, and resurrection. Beginning at sunset on Thursday and ending at sunset on Easter, the Triduum is the most important festival of the church year.

The color we use throughout Lent is violet, indicating a time of repentance, and we use red on Passion/Palm Sunday. Simplification of decorations in the sanctuary and prayer spaces visually expresses Lent. Candlesticks and crosses may be made of simple wood. Banners and vestments are often simple in design and material. We omit "Alleluias" from songs and prayers during Lent.

After the preparation and anticipation of the Lenten season, the Easter season begins with the celebrations of the Easter Vigil and Easter Sunday liturgies. Easter is more than a day-long celebration: Easter lasts fifty days as we celebrate the joy of being people of the resurrection. We are immersed ever more deeply into the mystery of Christ.

Paschal Mystery

Conversion: A Church Task

On the First Sunday of Lent each year, we each personally listen anew to our call to conversion. In *Catechism of the Catholic Church* #1428, we are reminded that conversion is not only for individuals but is also a task for the whole church. This is defined in *Dogmatic Constitution on the Church* (*Lumen Gentium*); give examples for each of the following points in #8 and #3.

1. The church is to proclaim by example humility and self-denial.

2. The church embraces with love all who are poor and who suffer.

CHRIST'S CALL TO CONVERSION CONTINUES

3. The church holds sinners dearly to itself.

4. The church, in constant need of purification, is always on the path of penance and renewal.

Palm Cross Instructions

The palm is the symbol of Palm Sunday.

Practice making palm cross to share with someone unable to come to Sunday worship.

Materials for One Palm Cross

◾ a ruler

◾ 1 strip of green construction paper 12 inches long and ½ inch wide

◾ 1 strip of green construction paper 14 inches long and slightly narrower than ¼ inch wide

Instructions

1. Use a ruler to measure and make marks on the shorter strip at ½ inch, 1 inch, 1½ inches, 3¾ inches, and 8 inches.

2. Fold the strip of construction paper at each mark as indicated. Flatten to form the crossbeam (which should be in the center).

3. Tuck the end of the longer strip between the small folds in the crossbeam, letting it stick out just a little bit. Hold firmly.

4. Loop the other end of the longer strip all the way around the crossbeam so the two ends of the longer strip touch. Slide the strip through the small fold, using the little bit of the first end to help keep the second on the outside as it goes through the fold.

5. Pull the strip all the way through so the crossbeam is secure.

6. Make a mark on the strip about 2½ inches from the crossbeam and fold. Push the long end through the small fold to make the long beam of the cross. Leave 2½ inches at the top of the cross.

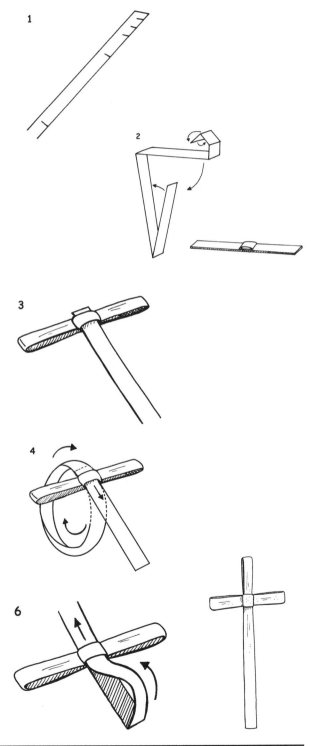

Mission Support

Many organizations offer resources for justice and mission awareness. These organizations offer a variety of materials, newsletters, magazines, videos, and guidelines. An organization involved in missionary activity usually also seeks ways to promote justice for all. The two efforts go hand in hand.

Columban Fathers

Mission Education Office
St. Columbans, NE 68056
Telephone: (402) 291-1920
Website: http://st.columban.org
E-mail: dove@columban.org

The Columbans offer numerous webpages that address justice education. Find information about their newsletter and a complete mission awareness program that includes videos, handouts, and a catechist guide, all available on free loan.

Catholic Relief Services

PO Box 17090
Baltimore, MD 21203-7090
Donor Services: (888) 277-7575
Website: www.crs.org/
E-mail: webmaster@crs.org

Catholic Relief Services offers numerous webpages that address justice education. They publish a magazine-type newsletter. Operation Rice Bowl is a complete program that gets children involved in global concerns, and special programs are available for youth.

Claretian Publications

205 W. Monroe St.
Chicago, IL 60606
Telephone: (800) 328-6515
Website: www.claretians.org

Claretian Publications offers a website that provides background information on global issues and social justice awareness. Magazine subscriptions, *At Home With Our Faith,* and materials for parents are available, and they also provide Hispanic ministry resources.

Maryknoll Fathers and Brothers

PO Box 304
Maryknoll, NY 10545-0304
Telephone: (914) 941-7590
Website: society.maryknoll.org
E-mail: mkweb@maryknoll.org

Maryknoll offers numerous webpages that address justice and mission education. A multitude of resources are available: magazines and study guides, an annual student essay contest, visuals, and guest speakers.

Salesian Missions

2 Lefevre Lane
PO Box 30
New Rochelle, NY 10802-0030
Telephone: (888) 608-2327
Website: www.salesianmissions.org
E-mail: info@salesianmissions.org

The Salesian Missions offer numerous webpages for global and mission awareness including a slide show and online visits to a multitude of countries. Magazines and videos are available.

Paschal Mystery

The Scrutinies

The First Scrutiny Ritual

Through ritual prayer, the Elect, those preparing for baptism, are called to scrutinize their ways of living. Community members pray with them and also scrutinize themselves as Christian models for the new members. The following is the format for the rite for the first scrutiny:

1. The readings for the Third Sunday of Lent Year A are proclaimed during liturgy.

The story of the woman at the well speaks of living water, that those who receive this water will never thirst. The Elect will soon approach the waters of baptism and new ways of life.

2. The presider asks the community to pray that the Elect will have a spirit of repentance and come to know freedom as members of God.

While praying for the Elect, the community members reflect on their own awareness of sin, the call to repentance, and what it means to be children of God.

3. The godparents place their right hands on the Elects' shoulders. The presider leads prayers of intercession for the Elect. Through these prayers the community asks that the Elect be led to complete their preparation and find Christ in the sacraments and that the Holy Spirit will help them.

Through these prayers the Elect and the whole assembly are strengthened.

4. An exorcism follows. First the presider prays to God to protect the Elect from selfishness and the power of Satan. In silent ritual the presider then lays hands on each member of the Elect. In the final prayer, the presider addresses Jesus, asking that the Elect be free from sin as they come to know living water.

As the Elect approach the time of their baptisms, they break away from the power of Satan. The prayers of the community have a greater pull than the powers of evil.

5. The Elect are dismissed to go in peace.

The Elect go out to reflect on the word of God and are assured of loving support.

The Second Scrutiny Ritual

For the second time, the Elect, those preparing for baptism, come before the community. Prayers help the Elect scrutinize their ways of living and receive the support of the community. Through these prayers we also evaluate how we carry out the mission of Jesus. The following is the format for the rite for the second scrutiny:

1. The readings for the Fourth Sunday of Lent Year A are proclaimed during liturgy.

The story of the man born blind enlightens us about how Jesus heals us and is our source of light, enabling the faithful to see. The Elect are learning to see in new ways to follow the light of Jesus.

2. The presider asks the community to pray that the Elect will have a spirit of repentance and come to know freedom as members of God.

While praying for the Elect, the community members reflect on their own awareness of sin, the call to repentance, and what it means to be children of God.

3. The godparents place their right hands on the Elects' shoulders. The presider leads prayers of intercession for the Elect. Through these prayers the community asks that the Elect remain faithful, boldly giving witness to the faith, and be enlightened by the Holy Spirit. The assembly also prays for those persecuted for Christ and for the whole world.

While praying for the Elect with these prayers, the assembly members renew their own faith and trust and evaluate their values compared to those of the world.

4. An exorcism follows. First the presider prays to God to free the Elect from false values and anything that blinds them to the truth. In silent ritual the presider then lays hands on each member of the Elect. In the final prayer, the presider asks Jesus to wake in the Elect a desire for good and to help them to see truth through the Holy Spirit.

As the Elect move closer to the time of their baptisms, they are guided away from error, doubt, and unbelief.

5. The Elect are dismissed to go in peace.

The Elect go out to reflect on the word of God and are assured of loving support.

The Third Scrutiny Ritual

For the third time, the Elect, now close to baptism, come before the community. Prayers help the Elect scrutinize their ways of living and receive the support of the community. With them, the other community members evaluate how well they carry out Jesus' mission. The following is the format for the rite for the third scrutiny:

1. The readings for the Fifth Sunday of Lent Year A are proclaimed during liturgy.

The story of Lazarus helps the Elect and assembly confront the reality of earthly death and realize that true life is with Christ. In entering the baptismal waters, the Elect die with Christ to be reborn with Christ.

2. The presider asks the community to pray that the Elect will have a spirit of repentance and come to know freedom as members of God.

While praying for the Elect, the community members reflect on their own awareness of sin, the call to repentance, and what it means to be children of God.

3. The godparents place their right hands on the Elects' shoulders. The presider leads prayers of intercession for the Elect. In these prayers the community asks that the Elect conform to Christ's Passion and resurrection. The assembly asks that they be strengthened by the example of those who have died for their faith. All offer prayers for those saddened by the deaths of loved ones.

While praying for the Elect with these prayers, the assembly members renew their own hope in the resurrection and seek to conform more closely to Christ.

4. An exorcism follows. First the presider prays to God to free the Elect from the death-dealing power of the spirit of evil and that they may live as witnesses in Christ. The presider lays hands on each member of the Elect and asks Jesus to free them from death through the power of the Holy Spirit.

As the Elect approach the time of their baptisms, they are guided away from error, doubt, and unbelief.

5. The Elect are dismissed to go in peace.

The Elect go out to reflect on the word of God and are assured of loving support.

Stations for Today

Station 1: Jesus Is Condemned to Death

Leader: *Pilate, with the power of life or death over another, submits to those who say, "Crucify him."*

Reader 1: We see Christ in today's world as we wait in hope with those imprisoned in the United States and throughout the world. We pray for an end to the death penalty and the useless ending of life. We hold fast to our belief in repentance and the forgiveness of sins.

Leader: We adore you, O Christ, and we bless you.

All: Because by your holy cross, you redeemed the world.

Station 2: Jesus Takes Up His Cross

Leader: *Accepting the inevitable, Jesus takes up the cross and beckons to others, saying, "Follow me."*

Reader 2: We see Christ in today's world as earthquakes, wars, tidal waves, floods, and other disasters befall people, and communities pull together the pieces of their lives. We pray that the world sees the crosses others are forced to carry and that those more fortune will feel compelled to help others.

Leader: We adore you, O Christ, and we bless you.

All: Because by your holy cross, you redeemed the world.

Station 3: Jesus Falls the First Time

Leader: *Jesus falls from the crushing weight of the cross, but he prays and gets back on his feet.*

Reader 3: We see Christ in today's world as people suffer crushing blows to their ways of life. Many fall from strokes and accidents, debilitating diseases, and financial setbacks. We pray with those who struggle up the stairway of recovery.

Leader: We adore you, O Christ, and we bless you.

All: Because by your holy cross, you redeemed the world.

Station 4: Jesus Meets His Mother

Leader: *His mother looks on in grief, accepting what she cannot change.*

Reader 4: We see Christ in today's world as mothers grieve the loss of children who die, whether they are lost to violence, malnutrition, disease, or abortion. We pray with all mothers who feel the pain of emptiness in their hearts.

Leader: We adore you, O Christ, and we bless you.

All: Because by your holy cross, you redeemed the world.

Station 5: Simon of Cyrene Helps Jesus

Leader: *Simon of Cyrene, unwillingly yet willingly, offers Jesus courage and renewed strength as he helps carry the cross.*

Reader 5: We see Christ in today's world as millions in our country and throughout the world notice the crosses of others. With generous donations, countless agencies can offer relief and seek justice. We pray for the success of Catholic Relief Services, Maryknoll Missionaries, and all others who strive to help those who suffer.

Leader: We adore you, O Christ, and we bless you.

All: Because by your holy cross, you redeemed the world.

Station 6: Veronica Wipes the Face of Jesus

Leader: *Veronica has the courage to defy the Romans to bring a breath of relief to Jesus' misery.*

Reader 6: We see Christ in today's world as people doing hospital and hospice work wipe the faces of those who are dying. We pray with those who defy criticism from others to minister to those with AIDS, bringing moments of relief from their suffering.

Leader: We adore you, O Christ, and we bless you.

All: Because by your holy cross, you redeemed the world.

Station 7: Jesus Falls a Second Time

Leader: *Jesus, weakened from being whipped, falls again.*

Reader 7: We see Christ in today's world in those in Iraq and Afghanistan who have collapsed under the heavy load of war. We pray for the innocent victims of war and a change of heart for perpetrators.

Leader: We adore you, O Christ, and we bless you.

All: Because by your holy cross, you redeemed the world.

Station 8: Jesus Speaks to the Women

Leader: *The women rend their garments and cry in grief for Jesus, yet he reaches out to console them.*

Reader 8: We see Christ in today's world as women, deprived of full dignity, suffer throughout the world. In many countries women do not have protection under the law; in other countries they continue to be demeaned by structural barriers formed over the millennia. We pray for full and equal treatment for all women everywhere.

Leader: We adore you, O Christ, and we bless you.

All: Because by your holy cross, you redeemed the world.

Station 9: Jesus Falls the Third Time

Leader: *Jesus falls again and again until he is unable to pull himself up.*

Reader 9: We see Christ in today's world as millions of people in Africa, displaced by war, fall and struggle to get up again and again. We pray for all those in Sudan, Angola, Senegal, Rwanda, and countless other places who have lost their homes to civil war.

Leader: We adore you, O Christ, and we bless you.

All: Because by your holy cross, you redeemed the world.

Station 10: Jesus Is Stripped

Leader: *Jesus' dignity is assaulted as he is stripped of his clothing.*

Reader 10: We see Christ in today's world as millions of the nation's poor seek food and shelter daily. We pray for those who suffer economic hardships, stripped of their jobs, their homes, their ability to provide food and clothing for their families, and their dignity.

Leader: We adore you, O Christ, and we bless you.

All: Because by your holy cross, you redeemed the world.

Station 11: Jesus Is Nailed to the Cross

Leader: *Jesus is painfully pierced by the nails.*

Reader 11: We see Christ in today's world as veterans of conflicts in Vietnam, the Balkans, the Persian Gulf, Iraq, and Afghanistan return to their homes in the United States and throughout Europe. Many of their lives have been "pierced" by chemical and trauma-induced ailments. We pray for those inflicted with lives of trauma.

Leader: We adore you, O Christ, and we bless you.

All: Because by your holy cross, you redeemed the world.

Station 12: Jesus Dies on the Cross

Leader: *Jesus dies at the hands of those who unjustly use their power.*

Reader 12: We see Christ in today's world as the families of the church women slain in El Salvador continue to mourn their loved ones, Sisters Dorothy Kazel, Ita Ford, and Maura Clarke and lay worker Jean Donovan. We pray for a conversion for all who use power unjustly.

Leader: We adore you, O Christ, and we bless you.

All: Because by your holy cross, you redeemed the world.

Station 13: Jesus Is Removed from the Cross

Leader: *Joseph of Arimathea, a distinguished member of the council, takes Jesus' body, wraps it, and lays it in the tomb.*

Reader 13: We see Christ in today's world as members of various Christian denominations throughout the world strive for oneness. We pray for ways to wrap all Christians believers in the cloak of unity and for ways to remove the obstacles that divide the Body of Christ.

Leader: We adore you, O Christ, and we bless you.

All: Because by your holy cross, you redeemed the world.

Station 14: Jesus Is Placed in the Tomb

Leader: *Joseph lays the body of Jesus in the tomb as Mary Magdalene and the other Mary sit and wait.*

Reader 14: We see Christ in today's world as families in Afghanistan, Iraq, and many countries in Africa bury their loved ones, who are too often under the age of seventeen. We pray for all those who fight and die for political freedom and for those in government who deny that freedom.

Leader: We adore you, O Christ, and we bless you.

All: Because by your holy cross, you redeemed the world.

Station 15: Resurrection

Leader: *Jesus rises from the dead and first appears to Mary Magdalene.*

Reader 15: We see Christ in today's world as many come to know the joy of resurrection. Inspired by a "Jubilee Year" attitude, much has already been accomplished for the poor and needy in this twenty-first century. We pray that the spirit of Jubilee continues so that millions more can start their lives anew.

Leader: We adore you, O Christ, and we bless you.

All: Because by your holy cross, you redeemed the world.

Community Reconciliation Service

Gathering

Sing "Change Our Hearts" from *Breaking Bread.*

Leader: May the peace of Christ be with you.
All: And also with you.
Leader: As we pray for repentance today, reflect on ways you might change to live fully as Christ wants. O God, you look on us with kindness and mercy. In your compassion grant us pardon from our sins.

Readings

First Reading: Baruch 1:15–22
Psalm Response: Have mercy, O God, and cleanse us from sin (adapted from Psalm 51:1,6,10,12).

Have mercy on me, O God, according to your steadfast love;
according to your abundant mercy, blot out my transgression. (*Response*)

You desire truth in our inward being,
therefore, teach me wisdom in my secret heart. (*Response*)

Then I will teach transgressors your ways,
and sinners will return to you. (*Response*)

Restore to me the joy of your salvation,
and sustain in me a willing spirit. (*Response*)

Gospel: Matthew 9:9–13

Short Homily / Reflection

- Jesus came to call sinners.
- Jesus came to save us from our sinfulness.
- God's mercy is all encompassing.
- No sin is unforgivable for those who are repentant.
- As a community, we should forgive others with the same unconditional forgiveness God offers us.
- We celebrate with those who turn away from sin.

Examination of Conscience

- What interests do I sometimes put before what is God's will?
- How can I make Sunday a more holy day of worship?
- How do I use my voice in unkind ways?
- How can I show more respect for the wisdom of elders?
- What did I do or say that hurt someone?
- How can I show respect for the gifts of creation?
- To what extent do I participate in the decadent sexual values of society?
- When have I been jealous of a person's material things?
- How can I bring more love into my home?

Act of Repentance

Response: God of mercy, strengthen us.

God of mercy, help us to turn away from sin. (*Response*)
Let us show true sorrow and make up for our sins. (*Response*)
Help us to be strong leaders of peace in our homes and world. (*Response*)
At home and at work, show us how to be more understanding. (*Response*)
Make us people of love and peace. (*Response*)

Act of Contrition

Together pray a form familiar to all, or have the participants repeat the following line by line:

My God, I am sorry for my sins with all my heart.
In choosing to do wrong and failing to do good,
I sin against you,
whom I should love above all things.
I firmly intend, with your help, to do penance, to sin no more,
and to avoid whatever leads me to sin.
Our savior Jesus Christ suffered and died for us.
In his name, my God, have mercy. Amen.

Individual Confession Option

With priests available and with option of a screen , penitents may go to private confession.

Quiet Reflection Option

Leader: Reflect quietly on ways you can turn away from the power of sin. (*Pause for a moment of silence.*)

Closing Prayer

Leader: Blessed are all who know the love and forgiveness of God. Proclaim God's mercy to all the world. Rejoice and go in peace.

Breaking Open Scripture Year A: Gifts of the Spirit

Proclaim 1 Corinthians 12:3–13 and John 20:19–23. In small groups discuss the following:

■ What do these Scriptures reveal about the Holy Spirit?

■ What does it mean to have each of the following gifts?

wisdom

knowledge

faith

healing

miracles

prophecy

discernment

speaking in tongues

understanding tongues

Breaking Open Scripture Year B: Fruits of the Spirit

Proclaim Galatians 5:22–25 and John 16:12–15. In small groups discuss the following:

■ What attributes do we display when we live by the Spirit?

■ Which of the following fruits of the Spirit is ripe and plump in you?

love

joy

peace

patience

kindness

generosity

faithfulness

gentleness

self-control

■ Which fruit of the Spirit needs to develop more in you?

■ Which fruits of the Spirit do you see ripening in this faith community?

Breaking Open Scripture Year C:
Names for the Holy Spirit

Proclaim Romans 8:8–17 and John 14:23–27. In small groups discuss the following:

■ What does it mean to be children of God?

■ What are some other names for the Holy Spirit?

■ Which one has the most meaning for you?

■ Why does God give us the Holy Spirit?

■ How does the Spirit wipe away fears?

■ What does each name for the Holy Spirit indicate about how the Spirit works among us?

"Welcome" in Various Languages

Cut out and glue each section onto an individual card.

Hebrew Shalom (*sha-LOHM*)	**French** Bonjour (*bohn-ZHOOR*)	**Hmong** Rua (*RU-ah*)
Spanish Bienvenidos (*BE-en-ven-ee-dos*)	**German** Guten Tag (*GOOT-en Tahk*)	**Portuguese** Boa Vinda (*BO-uh VIN-duh*)
Greek Kalimera (*kah-lee-MEH-rah*)	**Arabic** Al Salaam a'alaykum (*ahl sah-LAHM ah ah-LAY-koom*)	**Hawaiian** Heahea (*HEAH-heah*)
Italian Boun giorno (*bwohn JOR-noh*)	**Sign Language** Move your right hand away from your forehead and down, similar to saluting.	

Hebrew Shalom (*sha-LOHM*)	**French** Bonjour (*bohn-ZHOOR*)	**Hmong** Rua (*RU-ah*)
Spanish Bienvenidos (*BE-en-ven-ee-dos*)	**German** Guten Tag (*GOOT-en Tahk*)	**Portuguese** Boa Vinda (*BO-uh VIN-duh*)
Greek Kalimera (*kah-lee-MEH-rah*)	**Arabic** Al Salaam a'alaykum (*ahl sah-LAHM ah ah-LAY-koom*)	**Hawaiian** Heahea (*HEAH-heah*)
Italian Boun giorno (*bwohn JOR-noh*)	**Sign Language** Move your right hand away from your forehead and down, similar to saluting.	

Pentecost People Background Information

Easter is more than a day-long celebration: Easter lasts fifty days, so the church names the seven Sundays during the season as "Sundays *of* Easter" rather than "Sundays *after* Easter." During this period we gather to hear stories of the risen Christ. We are revitalized in remembering the growth and the struggles of the early church, and we reflect again on the impact this joyous news has on our lives and our life together. The color of this festive season is white to denote our great joy.

Forty days after Easter, the church celebrates the ascension of Jesus. We celebrate the feast of the Ascension on the Thursday after the Sixth Sunday of Easter or on the following Sunday. The Easter season closes with the feast of Pentecost, the fiftieth day, when we recognize and give thanks for God's gift of the Spirit to the church. The color for the day is red, which is the color for the festival of the Spirit.

Jesus loved the disciples with a love that grew during years of close living, tested by human foibles and miracles. Jesus' unconditional love was born of compassion and human understanding. When he was about to leave, Jesus promised to send a special gift to the disciples — the Spirit. The Gospel writers recount that on Pentecost the Spirit appeared passionately and with a loud noise in the guise of wind and fire. The Spirit consumed the disciples with the love of Jesus. The same Spirit is our gift. As Christians, we live the spirit of Pentecost year-round. In fact, what is Ordinary Time for Catholics is called the "season of Pentecost" in the common lectionary that many Christian denominations use.

People filled with the Spirit live in different ways from others. With lives directed by prayer and the messages of the Scriptures, disciples are aware of the power of forgiveness as one in the Body of Christ. Those filled with the Spirit have hope in eternal life and work for justice in this world to encourage that hope for those who are most in need.

Acts 2:1–11

While Pentecost was a special event for the Christian community, the Spirit of God had been present at creation (Gen 1:2), and as the early Christians knew, through ancient leaders such as David (Acts 1:16) and Isaiah (Acts 28:25). In addition, people believed that on a special day, God's Spirit would pour out on humankind in a special way (Joel 3:1–2). In Acts Peter identified the coming of the Holy Spirit at Pentecost as a fulfillment of that prophecy (Acts 2:16–17). The Spirit of God is the force that created and continues to create the world. God is the source of life for all the earth's creatures; God's breath animates the world.

The day of Pentecost was observed in the Jewish tradition fifty days (seven weeks) after Passover. The Pentecost festival, also known as the Feast of Weeks (sometimes called *Shavuot*), was originally an agricultural festival to celebrate the first harvest (Ex 23:14–17 and 34:18–24). In the first century, Pentecost was a festival that celebrated the gift of God's law to Israel. This celebration was the reason for the large number of Jews in Jerusalem (Acts 2:5).

Acts 2:1–11 is one description of the coming of the Spirit (see John 20:19–23 for another). Its strong metaphoric language — powerful wind, tongues of fire, and strange utterances — suggests a deeply dramatic experience for those gathered.

Wind and fire are signs of God's presence (Ex 3:2, Lev 9:24, 2 Sam 22:16, Job 37:10, Ezek 13:13). At Pentecost the sound of mighty wind conveyed the uncontrollable power of God. Fire reminded them of the divine presence, a presence that both illumines and purifies what it touches. Flames shaped like tongues revealed a divine presence connected to the power to witness. God was present in a powerful way as the Holy Spirit brought about the formation of the community of faith whose mission was to preach the good news.

The Spirit enabled the disciples to communicate with people who gathered in Jerusalem for the Pentecost celebration. The coming of the Holy Spirit served to unify those who were dispersed and divided by language. Each person recognized the message of the good news and the Spirit in which it was given.

John 20:19–23

This reading is another version of the gift of the Spirit. In John this gift occurred on Easter Sunday evening. The gift of the Holy Spirit is associated with the departure of Jesus (Jn 16:7). The Spirit is the link between Jesus' followers and the Creator. John the Baptist promised that Jesus would baptize with the Spirit (1:33), and the Easter evening encounter is this baptism.

Jesus greeted his disciples by saying, "Peace be with you" (20:19), a sign of the Spirit's presence. The sight of the risen Jesus filled them with joy (v 20), another witness to the Spirit. Jesus then commissioned his friends with the task he began. Throughout the Gospel Jesus spoke of himself as the one sent by God (5:36; 6:29; 17:3). His followers took on this role in the world. They were sent by Jesus to bring people to faith.

Like the breath of God at creation, Jesus breathes new life into the disciples. He gives them the power to forgive sin through the Spirit. Forgiveness and reconciliation are the ultimate signs of the transforming presence of the Spirit.

Easter Symbols Mean Justice

Pentecost people are symbolizing people. In prayer we engage in symbols to become more of what we are — people of justice.

- building a fire (matches in a small hibachi with crumpled paper)

- telling a story of faith (Bible)

- calling by name (saints book)

- waters of baptism (water in clear bowl)

- clothed in white for new life (white clothing)

- anointing with chrism (scented oil)

- laying on of hands (use your own hands)

- eucharistic bread, broken and shared (bread)

- eucharistic cup poured out (wine in a cup)

Prepare an exercise for the rest of the group to engage them in the symbols in ways that call believers to do justice. Use the following as hints:

- Fire purges wrongs done.

- Many Bible stories, such as Deuteronomy 15, are about the forgiveness of debt and treatment of needy neighbors.

- Many saints brought about changes for the poor.

- Baptism is a call to justice as we enter the waters and become one with Christ.

- All who are clothed in Christ are equal.

- We are anointed to service.

- We reach out a helping hand to others.

- We share what we have.

- We pour out ourselves for others without limit.

The Process

To create a prayer, write down the words, and describe the actions to engage people in the symbols. Design a prayer that will call people to a deeper awareness of how the Spirit moves us to justice.

An Enactment of Ezekiel 37:1–14

Assign each participant a part. Those who are willing to act will begin by being the "bones" and sit in "down" positions, such as on the floor with their heads drooped, kneeling while leaning against a wall, or in some other position that shows lifelessness. Other members will use shakers or maracas to replicate the rattling of bones. One person plays Ezekiel and moves among the group with long silky scarves or wide ribbons. Ezekiel may memorize the part or hold a Bible open to Ezekiel 37:4–7. Ask one person to narrate the following:

The hand of the God came upon me, brought me out by the Spirit of God, and set me down in the middle of a valley. It was full of bones. (*Ezekiel dramatically enters and walks among the "bones," looking down while shaking the head.*)

The hand of the God led me all around the bones. Very many were lying in the valley, and they were very dry. The hand of the God said to me, "Mortal, can these bones live?"

I answered, "O God, only you know." (*Ezekiel repeats, "O God, only you know."*)

Then the hand of the God said to me, "Prophesy to these bones. Say to them, 'O dry bones, hear the word of God. Thus says God to these bones: I will cause breath to enter you, and you shall live. I will lay sinews on you, cause flesh to come upon you, cover you with skin, and put breath in you, and you shall live. You shall know that I am God.'" (*Ezekiel repeats, "O dry bones, hear the word of God. Thus says God to these bones: I will cause breath to enter you, and you shall live. I will lay sinews on you, cause flesh to come upon you, cover you with skin, and put breath in you, and you shall live. You shall know that I am God." Ezekiel moves among the "bones," draping the scarves or ribbons over each person's shoulders. The bones begin to move joints.*)

I prophesied as I was commanded; and as I prophesied, suddenly there was a noise, a rattling, and the bones came together, bone to its bone. (*Ezekiel goes around touching the ribbons and looking carefully at the "bones."*)

I looked and there were sinews on them, and flesh had come upon them, and skin had covered them; but there was no breath in them.

Then the hand of the God said to me, "Prophesy to the breath, prophesy, mortal, and say to the breath: 'Thus says God: Come from the four winds, O Spirit of breath, and breathe upon these slain, that they may live.'" (*Ezekiel repeats, "Thus says God: Come from the four winds, O Spirit of breath, and breathe upon these slain, that they may live."*)

I prophesied as the hand of God commanded me, and the breath came into them, and they lived and stood on their feet, a vast multitude. (*The "bones" come to life, twirling their ribbons.*)

Then the hand of God said to me, "Mortal, these bones are the whole house of Israel. They say, 'Our bones are dried up, and our hope is lost; we are cut off completely.' Therefore, prophesy and say to them, 'Thus says God: I will open your graves and bring you up from your graves, O my people; and I will bring you back to the land of Israel. And you shall know that I am God when I open your graves and bring you up from your graves, O my people. I will put my spirit inside you, and you shall live, and I will place you on your own soil; then you shall know that I, God, have spoken and will act," says God. (*Ezekiel repeats, "Thus says God: I will open your graves and bring you up from your graves, O my people; and I will bring you back to the land of Israel. And you shall know that I am God when I open your graves and bring you up from your graves, O my people. I will put my spirit inside you, and you shall live, and I will place you on your own soil; then you shall know that I, God, have spoken and will act."*)

Pentecost Eggs

Prepare fun eggs for a Pentecost celebration.

Materials Needed for Resurrection Eggs

- large raw eggs

- confetti

- color tissue paper

- white glue

- wax crayons

- egg dye

Directions

For each raw egg, carefully cut off the end of the shell to create an opening to drain and refill the egg. Drain the egg from the shell, and thoroughly rinse the shell with hot water. Let the shell dry. Use wax crayons to write faith messages on the eggs. Color the eggshells with Easter egg coloring dye. Set each eggshell aside to dry (about ten minutes in the refrigerator dries the shells well). Stuff the eggshells with confetti until they are almost full. Use white glue to attach a small piece of color tissue paper over the opening and let it dry. On Pentecost a celebrator will break an egg over someone's head and say, "Rise to new life with the Spirit!"

Women of Faith Whom Jesus Knew

In the Sunday lectionary readings, we never hear many of the stories about Spirit-filled women. The significant verses about women in Scripture are often either omitted entirely or included only as an option.

In his encyclical *On the Dignity and Vocation of Women,* Pope John Paul II called for the recognition and appreciation of the historical gifts of women (#31). He recognized that the manifestations of the Spirit among women in history have been invaluable. He asked the church to recognize and appreciate the gifts of women for the common good of the church and of humanity.

Read the stories in your Bible to find out about the following women of faith:

- Shiphrah and Puah, two brave midwives, disobey the king to save a baby's life. See Exodus 1:8–22.

- Ruth refuses to desert her mother-in-law, Naomi, during a time of mourning and need. See Ruth 1:1–18

- Esther, a biblical heroine, saves her people from massacre. See Esther 7:1—8:2.

- Judith, a courageous heroine, risks her life with initiative and determination to save her people. See Judith 13:1–20.

- The Maccabee brothers' mother displays a valor worthy of everlasting remembrance. See 2 Maccabees 7:20–41.

- Mary of Bethany anoints Jesus at a banquet served by Martha in honor of Jesus. See John 12:1–8.

- Mary Magdalene, who was cured from illness, and Joanna, Susanna, and other women who assist Jesus from their own means, follow Jesus. See Luke 8:1–3.

- Jesus heals a man with a stoop. See Luke 13:10–17.

Spirit-filled Women of the Early Church

(information gleaned from Paul's letters and the Acts of the Apostles)

While the stories of many men, such as Paul, Stephen, and Barnabas, are recorded in detail and told in the lectionary readings during the Easter season, other men and women of the early church are not as familiar. The stories are not fully recorded, especially those of women, but they can be gleaned from Paul's letters and the Acts of the Apostles. The list below can help vivify the women's contributions to the early church. You may find parts of their stories in other passages beside those cited.

■ Prisca (also called Priscilla) and her husband, Aquila, were among the first Jewish Christians in Rome. An edict of Claudius forced them out of Rome. When they met Paul in Corinth, the three worked together as tentmakers. Priscilla and Aquila left Corinth with Paul, who separated from them at Ephesus. Priscilla and Aquila instructed a Jew named Apollos. He spoke with eloquence in fervently proclaiming the new way of God, so they clarified his knowledge. They also helped Timothy, who was the leader of the Ephesian community. Priscilla and Aquila evidently returned to Corinth to lead a house church as they are addressed in Paul's Letter to the Corinthians. They were eventually able to return to Rome and were leaders in bringing the Jewish and gentile Christians together. Paul recognized this pair for their devotion to spreading the Gospel, even to the point of risking their lives. (Acts 18:2–26; 1 Cor 16:19; Rom 16:3: 2 Tim 4:19)

■ Tabitha (also called Dorcas) continually performed deeds of kindness and charity while making tunics and other garments. She was held in high esteem in her community, and many widows were concerned when she became ill. Peter cured her and restored her to the faith community. (Acts 9:36–40)

■ Lydia of Thyatira, a dealer in fine purple woven cloth, opened her heart to accept the message proclaimed by Paul. She was baptized with her whole household and opened her home in hospitality to Paul's group. (Acts 16:13–15)

■ Junia, recognized by Paul as an outstanding apostle along with Andronicus, was imprisoned with Paul for love of the Gospel. Junia, from the Roman community, was one of the *very* first Christians. Her conversion to faith predates Paul's. (Romans 16:7)

■ Damaris, an Athenian woman, listened to Paul and became a believer. She joined Paul in ministry. (Acts 17:34)

■ Phoebe, a deacon of the church at Cenchreae, was a benefactor of many including Paul. Paul recognized her and introduced her as a saint. (Rom 16:1–3)

■ A woman named Mary was a hard worker for the faith in the Roman community. (Rom 16:6)

■ Tryphaena and Tryphosa were recognized by Paul as workers for Christ. (Rom 16:12)

■ Euodia and Syntyche, although they did not always agree about all things, worked beside Paul. He asked others to pray for them to have mutual understanding. (Phil 4:1–3)

■ Nympha, leader of a house church, received a letter from Paul to be read to the church gathered in her house in or near Laodicea. (Col 4:15–18)

As is true for the woman who anointed Jesus with oil (who Jesus said would never be forgotten), the names of many women who worked for the early church were never recorded. However, we can glean their stories from the few facts that we have. Below are some of the women who are not known by name but by the works they did for the sake of the good news:

■ Prominent women of Thessalonica took great risks to join the house church of Jason. Jason and those with him were made to pay fines after being unjustly accused of stirring up opposition to Caesar's decrees. (Acts 17:4–9)

■ The mother of Rufus was considered by Paul to be as his own mother. (Rom 16:13)

■ Four daughters of Philip the evangelist were gifted at proclaiming the word of God. (Acts 21:9)

In our discussions and Bible storytelling, let us keep in memory the names and works of those women, as well as men, who gave fully and generously to help spread the good news in early Christian times.

Noisemakers

The coming of the Spirit was accompanied by a large noise.

You can make fun and easy-to-make noisemakers using several different craft supplies.

Adults and older children can make them for young members of the community.

Use the following different ideas and instructions to make noisemakers:

Cardboard Tube Instrument

Materials for One Instrument

cardboard tube (large or small)
gravel fish tank rocks
2 large balloons
heavy-duty tape

Instructions

Decorate the cardboard tube with a nice design or color. Place a large balloon on one end of the tube, stretching the balloon to make it fit snugly. Use heavy-duty tape to secure the balloon on the tube. Put a handful of gravel into the open end of the tube (if it is a small tube; put in two handfuls for a larger tube). Put the second balloon over the other opening just as you did the first. Now you are ready to shake, shake, shake!

Finger Cymbals

Materials for One Set of Cymbals

2 metal lids of the same size
½-inch wide elastic
hammer
nail

Instructions

Cut two 4-inch pieces of elastic. Use the hammer and nail to punch a hole in the center of each lid. Push each end of a piece of elastic through a hole. Tie the ends of the elastic into a knot. Slip your finger cymbals onto your thumb and pointer finger and bang them together!

Paper Plate Shaker

Materials for One Paper Plate Shaker

2 paper plates
stapler
tape
small craft bells

Instructions

Decorate the outside bottom of each plate with a nice design or color. Put one plate face-up, and fill the center with small craft bells. Put the other plate on top, and staple the edges shut. Make sure to place the staples close enough together so the bells do not fall out. Place a piece of tape over each staple for safety. Now make some noise!

Note: Instead of bells, use recycled bottle caps, gravel, or recycled nuts and bolts. Use aluminum pie tins instead of paper plates to make shinier and noisier instruments.

Film Container Noisemaker

Materials for One Noisemaker

1 film container with lid
hot glue
5 pennies
stickers, buttons, or other craft items

Instructions

Fill the container with the pennies, and use hot glue to attach the lid to the container. Decorate with stickers, buttons, or other craft items to make a nice design. Now shake away!

Pentecost People

The Spirit in Scripture

In Hebrew the feminine word ruah means "Spirit, wind, breath." Read the following passages,

and write each scriptural message about the Spirit in your own words:

GENESIS 1:1-2

ECCLESIASTES 12:7

PSALM 139:7-8

PSALM 31:5

JOEL 2:28-29

ACTS 2:17-18

ISAIAH 42:1

ISAIAH 61:1

LUKE 1:31-42

JOHN 4:24

JOHN 20:21-22

ACTS 7:55, 59

MATTHEW 5:3

LUKE 4:18

GALATIANS 5:2-23

1 THESSALONIANS 5:19

Appendix 2

Ministry Resource Sheets

The Lectionary and the Church Year

The lectionary is a cycle of Bible readings intended for liturgical use. The lectionary used in the Roman Catholic Church today, often called the Roman Lectionary, is part of the liturgical reform of Vatican Council II. The use of this particular lectionary is recent. Official use began on the First Sunday of Advent in 1969, with slight revisions in 1998. This "new" lectionary reintroduces the reading from the Old Testament as a consistent part of the Liturgy of the Word. It also gives a broader selection of the New Testament than was found prior to 1969.

A fixed cycle of biblical readings is neither new to our faith nor unique. Since ancient times synagogues have appointed designated Scripture readings for Jewish festivals and sabbaths. For instance, Jesus returned to his home town synagogue in Nazareth, and "the scroll of the prophet Isaiah was given to him" (Lk 4:16–17).

Over time the early church developed a pattern of readings. Readings became fixed for important feasts such as Easter. As liturgical seasons such as Lent developed, other readings became standardized. The "Ordinary" Sundays, Sundays not connected with either a feast or a season, were the last to acquire specific, regular readings.

The lectionary is organized in a three-year cycle: A, B, and C. Each year focuses on one of the synoptic Gospels. Year A uses the Gospel of Matthew; year B, the Gospel of Mark; and year C, the Gospel of Luke. Parts of the Gospel of John are proclaimed each year.

The church year begins each Advent and changes on the First Sunday of Advent. On feasts and major seasons of the church year, the three readings are related. During Ordinary Time only the first reading and the Gospel are purposely complementary. During Ordinary Time the second reading is a week-by-week walkthrough of one of the letters.

Lectionary for Masses with Children generally follows the Roman lectionary for the Sunday readings, although it often shortens the readings. Proclamations for children's Liturgy of the Word may come from either lectionary or a Bible.

The Church Year

The lectionary offers Bible passages that were chosen for the seasons of the church year and tell the story of Jesus' life and ministry. The highlight is the paschal mystery, Christ's death, resurrection, and imminent return.

■ In *Advent,* we prepare for the second coming of the Messiah and the celebration of Jesus' birth. The color violet expresses the mood of turning toward God with anticipation. We sometimes use blue-violet to reflect Mary's roll in salvation history.

■ At *Christmas,* we celebrate the incarnation and the coming of the Messiah as a historical person into our lives today and into a world of justice at the end of time. The color white reflects the mood of joy.

■ During *Ordinary Time,* between Christmas and Lent, we focus on Jesus' call of the disciples and healing ministry. The color green indicates that hope springs forth.

■ During *Lent,* we prepare, along with the catechumens, for the important days ahead. The color violet shows our penitential and pensive mood as we look ahead to the cycle of suffering, death, and resurrection.

■ During *Easter,* which lasts from Easter Sunday through Pentecost, we struggle with the mystery of the resurrection and the necessity of carrying on Jesus' work. The white color expresses a mood that is not the bubbly joy of the innocent but the deep joy of one who has seen suffering and death — and triumphed.

■ During the summer and fall of *Ordinary Time,* we again focus on the business of bringing Christ into the world in practical ways. The color green reminds us of the hope and responsibility of bringing social justice to the world.

Developing Bible Skills

Hearing Scripture proclaimed from the Bible is an important impetus for faith development. As we discuss what biblical stories might mean for us living in the twenty-first century, some people may ask, "What is the background of the Bible? From where did it come? How did it come to be in this particular form and translation?" Some faith members may have had little "hands-on" experience with the Bible and may feel embarrassed about this. Most will have a longing to "know" the Bible better to sense being part of the faith family.

It is important to explore questions about the Bible. While some Bible exercises are part of the catechetical sessions, ministers should help all of the faithful become more familiar with God's word.

Consider some of the following ideas to help you and others become more familiar with the history, structure, and content of the Bible. Be careful, however, not to impose explorations of the Bible. Wait for the participants' curiosity to be aroused and ask questions.

Use Bibles Whenever You Gather

We encourage members to read the Scriptures and familiarize themselves with the Bible. Present those in the initiation process, even young people, with their own Bibles (perhaps mentors could purchase the Bibles).

Become Familiar with the Bible

Review the order and grouping of the seventy-three books of the Bible by going through the entire book together. Together turn the pages from beginning to end, having the participants call out the names of the books that correspond to the groupings below. Invite everyone to share anything they have heard about these books, what they notice about their names and lengths, and so on. Discuss questions as they arise, and write down questions you need to research or discuss with someone such as a minister.

Old Testament: 46 books

- Books of the Law: 5 books
  (also called the Pentateuch or Torah)

- Books of History: 16 books

- Books of Wisdom and Poetry: 7 books

- Books of the Prophet: 18 books

New Testament: *27 books*

- The Gospels: 4 books

- Early Church History (Acts of the Apostles): 1 book

- Letters: 21 books

- Revelation: 1 book

The Testaments

Some Bible scholars, especially those in dialogue with Jewish leaders, object to the term "Old Testament" because it seems insensitive to Jews who believe the term implies that their Bible is out of date and has been replaced. Therefore, some Christian scholars and writers use the term "Hebrew Scriptures" instead of Old Testament. This term is problematic for Catholics, however, because the Catholic "Old Testament" includes seven books that, though reverenced by Jews, were not all written in Hebrew and are not part of the Jewish canon of the Bible (Baruch, Sirach, Wisdom, Judith, Tobit, and 1 and 2 Maccabees). Moreover, the lectionary includes many of these writings. Jewish people use the term *Tanakh,* an acronym for the Hebrew Bible based on the Hebrew initials for the text's parts: (1) The Torah is also known as the Law, the five books of Moses, or the Pentateuch; (2) *Nevi'im* means the Prophets; (3) *Ketuvim, Hagiographa,* means the Writings.

To avoid the controversy, it only takes a little time to get used to using "First Testament" and "Second Testament." Using "First Testament" instead of Old "Testament" does not imply that these books are out of date.

Experience of God

Talk with other ministers in your faith community about their understanding of nurturing faith. When we share our faith, the heart of our faith is our experience of God. We might use many different words, stories, gestures, and symbols to share that experience, but at the center is a belief that God, who is love, is real and active in our lives and our world.

We know that God is not one dimensional. The Bible has many different images for God: images that speak of king-like power and feminine wisdom, of being on high and lifted up yet closer to us than we are to ourselves. We know that God is so mysterious that no name can be used, and we call God by the most personal name, "Abba."

As people of faith, we experience God in many different ways. We use different images and metaphors to try to describe that experience to one another. No one image is the "right" one. Which of the following biblical images speak most clearly to you about your experience of God? Are there others you would add to the list? Which ones do you think will have the most significance for the members of your group?

Biblical Images of God

- a dove coming down from heaven
- a still, small voice; a whisper
- tongues of flame
- a rushing wind
- an eagle
- a woman in labor, crying out in pain
- a caring shepherd
- I AM
- a mother caring for her child
- one who suffers with humankind
- a rock, a fortress
- *El Shaddai:* God Almighty
- *El Elyon:* God Most High

- a woman searching for a coin that is lost
- a voice calling out your name
- truth
- a Spirit moving over the surface of the water
- a loving father
- a seeker of love and justice
- a faithful leader
- the creator and sustainer of the universe
- one who forgives
- the one who is love
- God who is revealed in Jesus Christ
- the beginning and the end

Nurturing Faith

What is the purpose of our work with adults, young people, and children? Why do we do what we do? Which of the following purpose statements is closest to your understanding of the purpose of religious formation? Would your statement be something completely different or perhaps a combination of parts of these?

The purpose of faith formation is ...

■ to come to know God, who is revealed in Jesus Christ and experienced through the Spirit, that we may be saved.

■ to connect the stories and symbols of our faith with life experience to live the way God would have us live.

■ to grow in love and knowledge of God, that we might become fully alive, working for justice and wholeness for all people (God's reign).

■ to share the tenets of our faith and hand on the tradition of our church.

■ to grow in mind, body, and spirit and in loving community with others.

■ to develop close relationships with God so we can love and serve others.

■ to share in the heritage and community of our faith so we may become the people God would have us be.

■ to move from brokenness to wholeness, from despair to hope, from lies to truth, from hate to love, and from doubt to faith.

■ to bring the good news to others and make God's reign present.

Knowing About God or Knowing God

Ministers have the responsibility of creating an atmosphere that enables people to grow in relationship with God. Faith is a response to a relationship with God. Through life experiences, beliefs may change and develop as we grow. Relationships with God can begin at anytime and will grow as people grow.

Unless people make the connection between what they hear about God and their everyday lives and develop a relationship with God, what they learn remains impersonal. Knowing *about* God is not the same as *knowing* God.

Whenever you meet with a group, take time for prayer, and provide experiences to help the people you work with feel the closeness of God, our creator, Jesus, our friend, and the Spirit, our comforter and life-giver. People often learn through relationships. Your presence and your modeling of caring may help them understand more of who God is and what God's love is like. Sharing from your heart and your commitment to be present are far more important than having all the "right" knowledge.

Facilitating Intergenerational Groups

When sharing faith with groups of all or any ages, consider the following guidelines:

■ Speak in a manner that is neither condensing to adults nor over the heads of younger members.

■ Say what you believe, and be yourself. When you are not sure or wonder about a particular faith issue, share your questions and ask the person what he or she thinks.

■ While leading groups as a representative of the church, take caution not to teach personal beliefs or faith practices as if they were doctrine.

■ Tell stories, including your own, without telling anyone what they should think, feel, or believe.

■ Carefully listen to what others share.

■ Develop a personal sense of God's presence through regular prayer or meditation.

■ Provide a variety of activities that meet the needs of adults and children. Do not expect adults to act like children or children to act like adults.

Try to create an atmosphere in which everyone does the following:

■ feels at home, accepted, and free to ask questions.

■ wants to share their talents and skills in the service of others.

■ feels God's Spirit at work in the ups and downs of the people around them.

■ is encouraged to develop prayer lives and personal relationships with God.

Ways to Build Trust

- Always be positive. Try to help each member feel cared about.

- Talk to people at their level. Eye contact is very important. When a person is seated or when talking with small children, bend down, kneel, or sit.

- Be consistent about your expectations and guidance. Be positive, gentle, pleasant, calm, firm, and sincere.

- Make a suggestion, not a command.

- Accept everyone's feelings as authentic. Listen to their explanations of how they feel, and never trivialize their ideas.

- Spotlight people's strengths. Help everyone shine at what they do best.

- Offer choices only when legitimate. Offer compromises or alternatives if needed.

- Set an example. Expect cooperation and express an openness to be cooperative with others.

- Establish a climate of mutual respect and trust. Be consistent and impartial. Make sure everyone is included and their opinions are valued.

- Celebrate individuality. Rather than treat differences as annoyances, look for the unique combination of qualities and characteristics of each person.

- Protect the rights of each member to be heard and to feel secure.

- Come well prepared. If you arrive half-prepared, the group members may feel that halfhearted attention is also acceptable. Structure and routine help create a positive environment.

- Use presence to affect behavior. Simply move to stand beside a person who is causing a distraction. Waiting in silence may help someone recognize that he or she is interrupting. When the member's attention returns, nod in a friendly way or say thanks and continue.

- Never publicly embarrass someone. If someone continually disrupts or dominates the group process, speak to the member in private. Look the person in the eye, and say how you feel the behavior affects the group. Use a calm voice and suggest an alternative.

- Add variety. Ask the members for ideas, and implement suggestions of others.

Shared Space

Most faith community ministries have to share space with the parochial school or other programs. Ministers often struggle to create privacy for their programs, storage for their supplies, and ways to remove everything easily. The following are a few tips for sharing space:

- Mount charts and visuals on posterboard that you can move from place to place.

- Use a portable clothesline and clothespins to hang pictures, posters, and art projects.

- Decorate a large box with a lid to hold all your supplies. Make sure it has handholds and you can carry it easily.

- Cover a pieces of corrugated cardboard with bright fabric for an improvised bulletin board.

- Slit a large refrigerator box down one side along the fold. Open it up and use it as a divider or a great wall.

- If chairs are in short supply, sit on carpet squares or remnants available at carpet dealers.

- Spread an old shower curtain on the floor for messy projects.

- Use tape on the floor as a visual: Use masking tape for games or to designate specific areas in a room. (*Caution:* Avoid hockey tape or duct tape because it takes off the surface of the floor. Also make sure to remove all the tape at the end of the day.)

- Always set up a simple prayer area. Have a candle in a holder, an attractive basket for an offering, and small color cloths for the various church seasons.

- Be creative with the participants, and help them feel comfortable in whatever space is available. One thing we can learn using portable spaces is that we experience God's community wherever we meet!

Intelligence Styles

Research tell us that there are seven or more "intelligences." We are all somewhat "intelligent" in all areas, but most of us have modalities that tend to work better for us when we process information. For example, some of us work well with words; others prefer logic and numbers; and others are good at music, art, drama, dance, or sports. Some people prefer working by themselves, while others work well with people.

Learning theories can be applied to faith development. Whatever your ministry, each member of your group will favor a particular intelligence style. Offer a wide variety of experiences during the year so each person has opportunities that favor their strengths as well as opportunities to experience other modalities.

Keep the following seven intelligences in mind when preparing to lead others.

Linguistic

(*use of language, both written and spoken*)

People who favor this style prefer thinking and processing through written and spoken words. They have the ability to memorize facts and enjoy reading. Activities that use this intelligence are discussion, reading, writing, oral presentations, and poetry.

Musical

(*use of pitch, rhythm, and songs*)

People who favor this style enjoy rhyme, rhythm, and repetition. Activities that use this intelligence are singing, playing instruments, listening to music, and writing songs.

Logical / Mathematical

(*use of abstract reasoning, sequences, and logical connections*)

People who favor this style enjoy thinking deductively and working with numbers. Activities that use this intelligence are puzzles, problem-solving or analytical tasks, and anything that involves figuring something out.

Spatial

(*use of visual images, pictures, and spatial skills*)

People who favor this style enjoy creating designs and visual images. Activities that use this intelligence are drawing, painting, sculpture, and the use of pictures, maps, and charts.

Kinesthetic

(*use of physical movement and coordination*)

People who favor this style enjoy body movement. Activities that use this intelligence are dance, mime, sports, and drama.

Interpersonal

(*use of group relationships and leadership skills*)

People who favor this style enjoy working together with other people. Activities that use this intelligence are group discussion, role-playing, small-group tasks, and teaching others a skill.

Intrapersonal

(*use of inner knowledge, self-awareness, and self-reflection*)

People who favor this style enjoy working alone. Activities that use this intelligence are journaling, meditation, and quiet reflection.

Creative Expression

Faith development depends on stimulation. For ministry formation and for whole-community faith formation, set up opportunities for the members to express themselves at specially designed centers. Provide materials they can use in creative expression to bring together the story of faith with their own experience. People become more committed and involved when they make their own choices. Their motivation increases when they can choose activities that match their own interests and abilities. Activity centers encourage effective and creative expression and provide opportunities for freedom of expression, personal interaction, and catering to a diversity of learning styles.

This approach often works well groups of various ages come together for a whole-community experience. Organize the centers and space carefully, and share the responsibility for the various centers to ensure that this format is a great success. This is not a quiet experience, so be creative and enjoy the energy and noise!

Activity Center Possibilities

The type of activities you plan depends on the theme and purpose. Provide at least two or three centers each time.

- *Snack Preparation Center:* This center works well whenever you plan activity center experiences. Use no-bake snack recipes, or arrange to use the church kitchen to bake bread or make cookies or muffins. Planning to offer recipes for foods eaten during biblical times is one possibility. Share food prepared in this center with the rest of the members or with the entire church community.
- *Drama Center:* Provide costumes and props for the group to re-enact biblical stories, have the members create plays based on a theme for the day. Try to provide time for the whole community to enjoy the dramatic presentations.
- *Puppet Center:* Have a variety of puppets available for enacting a known story or creating a new one. Also provide materials for the members to make their own puppets.
- *Paper and Pencil Center:* Provide materials for the members to respond to the story through word games, drawings, crossword puzzles, and so on.
- *Art Center:* Provide a variety of media so the members can respond to the story through paintings, drawings, murals, collages, and so on.
- *Game Center:* Create a floor-size game (for example, Snakes and Ladders), or provide cooperative board games.
- *Music Center:* Provide materials to make musical instruments to use while learning songs.
- *Exploring outside the Room:* A small group might visit another area of the church for a specific reason (for example, searching for Christian symbols) or take a short walk outside around the church property (for example, finding signs of new life).

Guidelines for Activity Centers

- Decide how to establish the centers: in different rooms? outside? in different sections of a large area?
- Select craft and activity projects that appeal to several age levels or levels of difficulty.
- Recruit adults or youth to assist in preparing for, supervising, and cleaning up the activity centers.
- Ensure that each activity leader gathers the needed supplies and prepares a sample of the project.
- Help activity leaders determine how many members each activity center can accommodate. A limited number of chairs at each center helps members identify when that center is full.
- Make signs for each activity center, with a title and the number of members the center can accommodate.
- Plan for all the participants to begin by gathering in one area. Have each activity leader introduce his or her center, show a sample, and state the limit of participants.
- Choose a method (for example, by age groups or birthday groups) for the members to make their first choices, varying this each time so everyone eventually has his or her first choice.
- If it is possible for the members to choose several centers, allow them the freedom to wander around to make their choices. Mention that if one center is full, they need to make other choices.
- Provide a quiet, supervised center with books and a play center with toys, play dough, and so on for young children who choose not to participate in the activity centers.

Note: It is important at the end of activity center time to gather together again and share what everyone did with one another (for example, through the puppet play they created, showing the artwork they did, or sharing the food they created). End with a song and/or prayer.

Art and Music

Art Tips

People often express their feelings and ideas through art. The process is more important than the product.

- Prepare all the supplies before the session. Provide skin-tone colors available from several companies in crayons, construction paper, markers, and tempera paint.
- Make a sample of any craft to become familiar with the process and to show as a model.
- Have supervisors to help during art time that involves children.
- To cut several items from a pattern, paper-clip several sheets of paper beneath the pattern and cut it out.
- Large glue sticks, which only cost a little more than small ones, are best and do not dry out quickly.
- Check with a printing shop for free scraps of color paper and cardboard.
- Cut holes in the lid of a candy box to hold paints so they do not tip over.
- For children, provide paint cover-ups such as the following:

    Cut off the collars and the bottom halves of the sleeves of discarded adult shirts, which children can wear backwards.

    Cut arm and head holes along the seams of old pillowcases, and then slip the open ends over the members' heads.

    Cut discarded shower curtains into appropriate-size ovals, each with a head hole in the center. Cutting holes cut for arms and the neck in plastic garbage bags also works.

Cleanup Tips

- Add a small amount of liquid detergent to tempera paint to make drips and spills easier to wipe up.
- Cover tabletops with newspapers or plastic cloths for rapid cleanup.
- Make sponge holders to keep paint jars from tipping. In the center of each sponge, cut a hole the size of a jar, and then fit the jars in the holes. The sponges keep the paint jars upright and also catch drips.
- Provide containers of soapy water for glue brushes or paintbrushes as the members finish with them.
- Have buckets of warm, soapy water and towels ready.

Making Music

Music is a universal language and integral to worship and prayer. Through music, people experience joy and creative expression. Music is an acceptable release and expression of feelings and emotions. It can quiet or calm people or soothe hurt and troubled feelings. Encourage participants to "put themselves" into music — to interpret music in their own styles and make up new words, new melodies, and new movements. Emphasize the member, not the leader, and the enjoyment, not the skill.

Singing Together

- "Share" a song rather than "teach" it. Know a song well yourself, and then sing it several times while the group listens. Do not teach a song by repeating words separate from the music.
- If a music minister is not available, play a recorded song to help the group learn it.
- Sing with enthusiasm; enunciate very clearly and use various ways to help others realize what the words mean so they find pleasure in singing and music.
- Use fingerplays or gestures to help members remember the words.
- Sing a song many times. Everyone enjoys the repetition of a delightful song.
- Encourage the members to add other words or verses.
- Do not pressure anyone to sing.
- Nearly all songs and music lend themselves to movement. Have the group stand for singing and move to the music.
- After the group learns a song, provide instruments (such as a guitar, autoharp, recorder, tambourine, piano, or homemade instruments) to accompany the singing, if possible.
- Improvise with homemade instruments. Use wooden spoons, coffee cans with lids, sleigh bells on elastic, or wooden blocks covered with sandpaper.
- Make rhythm instruments to celebrate special events and add dramatic expression.
- Offer maracas, triangles, and other instruments to various members scattered throughout the group to play during the singing.
- Use music as an opportunity for cross-cultural sharing. Use music from various ethnic groups in the community to foster worldwide solidarity.
- Do not apologize for your singing! Relax with the music, and do not be a perfectionist.

Working with Story and Symbol

A major part of our Judeo-Christian heritage is story: of our own human experiences and of God's presence and activity in the world. Appropriate story styles for these age levels include the following:

- *Personal Stories:* Share your own faith story and feelings, and encourage the participants to share theirs.
- *Stories in Character:* Use costumes or props to "become" a character.
- *Stories with Visuals:* Use pictures to present key images and explore what you can see and feel in the pictures.
- *Stories from Books:* Read or use stories that are particularly well told or have powerful illustrations.
- *Tell the Story Together:* If the biblical story is familiar, groups tell it in their own words using drama, role-playing, or puppets.

Storytelling Tips

- Telling a story in your own words is usually more effective than reading. The story must come through the teller. Use your voice, facial expressions, props, and so on.
- Maintain eye contact. Mark five or six key words in your notes, so you can see where you are at a glance.
- Ask some questions to keep the group involved.
- Visuals keep the participants focused and help them remember the story. Discuss the pictures and what is happening in them.
- Use humor, puns, cartoons, or your artistic ability. An overhead projector works well for telling a story through drawing. The light focuses attention.
- Storytelling is an art that grows through practice.

Dramatic Options for Storytelling

Everyone can enjoy the dramatization of Bible stories, the lives of the saints, and segments of church history. Members can perform for the group and for others with simple preparations or elaborate props and costumes if time and interest permit.

Play

Supplies: props, costumes (for example, bathrobes, towels, and ties), scripts or role cards

Discuss each of the characters, and plan how the participants will portray the characters. You might script the play or have the characters ad-lib conversations after the group decides the general direction of each conversation and the scenes to include. Encourage the participants to really "get to know" the characters they will play by thinking about what they look like, what they do, what is important to them, their names, and their ages. Prepare costumes and plan the props.

Puppet Play

Supplies: craft items, glue, scissors, scripts

For a puppet theater, use a large cardboard carton from which you cut a window or a table laid on its side.

Mime

Supplies: props, costumes (*optional*), script

One person reads dramatically, pausing at the appropriate moments, while others perform the actions. This form of drama often enables actors to enact everything including wind, trees, and other nonhuman parts of the story.

Photo Story

Supplies: instant-developing camera or digital camera with a printer, props, costumes, scripts, mural paper, markers

Create a still life of each main event in the story. Dress people as the characters in each scene, and arrange them in poses, with props, that depict that part of the story. Use an instant camera to take a picture of each main action or event. Arrange the pictures in order on a large sheet of mural paper, and write text for each scene of the story.

Video

Supplies: video camera, viewing equipment, props, costumes, scripts

Prepare the drama for a simple play, planning each scene. Videotape each main event of the drama in separate sections. Because you will only tape one section at a time, you have lots of time for costume changes. (People can play several characters; even "lead" characters can be used for crowd scenes.) You do not need scripts — the participants can memorize a short section at a time.

Radio Drama or Talk Show Interviews

Supplies: audiocassette player and tape, props to assist with sounds

This option requires sounds and speaking only. Discuss each character and the feelings they may have experienced in the story. How can someone express these feelings through words, voice inflections, and sounds? Discuss the actions and the sounds that might have accompanied the events. How can participants create these sounds? Script the play or ad-lib it after you decide the general direction for each scene.

Guiding Meditations

In our busy, noisy world, people need time for quiet. It is important to provide comfortable places where they can temporarily be alone in their own peace and quiet. In some homes, however, that is not always physically possible.

One way to help is to lead them through meditation into finding an inner quiet space. In this technique you take the participants into an imaginary situation, and encourage them to experience it. When you lead a guided meditation, the setting is important. It is best to use a room with carpet, cushions, and comfortable furniture and where you can dim the light. Encourage the group to find comfortable places by themselves or on the floor, relax their muscles, and close their eyes.

Start with simple breathing exercises. Ask everyone to be very quiet and listen to the rhythm of their own breathing. Suggest that everyone take a deep breath, leading by example, and exhale slowly. Repeat the exercise four or five times. When everyone is quiet, guide them through a short imaginary situation. Speak slowly in a calm voice, pausing between sections. Pause for a few moments of silence before, during, and after the meditation. As you come to the end of the meditation, ask everyone to open their eyes slowly when they are ready.

Some leaders tell us that they are surprised by how well their groups enter this experience.

Sample Guided Meditation

Based on Psalm 145

Begin with breathing exercises as outlined above. When the room is quiet and people seem relaxed and focused, proceed as follows:

You are standing on a mountain, so high up that you can see in all directions. Below you hills roll away into the distance.

Far away you can see the blue-green sea, stretching out to the sky beyond. You realize that you can strangely see details: a fox on a distant hillside, a butterfly in a field miles away.

You look deep into the sea, observing the many creatures that live there. As you look up into the sky, you see an eagle soaring, its wing feathers bright in the sun. What else can you see in the sky?

Looking higher you see the moon and then planets circling around a distant sun. All around you, as far as you can imagine, you see the wonderful things that God made.

You hear a voice singing a song that is older than the forests: "I will proclaim your greatness, O God. All your creatures will praise you."

Imaging

An extension of guided meditation is imaging, in which everyone creates their own situations in their minds. For example, begin an imaging exercise by asking everyone to relax and close their eyes. Invite them to visualize a peaceful scene. Pause for thirty seconds of silence. Ask them to add details to the scene, such as smells, sounds, sights, and colors. Pause for thirty seconds. Then Jesus appears in the scene with them and …. Pause for thirty seconds. Ask everyone to return to the present, and invite them to talk about what they imagined, if they wish. What did they see? smell? hear? do?

Meditations for Ministers

Patience

Dear God, the next time I stand impatiently
in front of a microwave oven wishing it would "hurry up,"
help me remember food cooked slowly over an open fire.
Help me remember people who have no food.
Teach me patience, God.
Remind me that growing up is a life-long process, and remind
me to feel grateful to be growing slowly in faith with others.
And God? Help me to remember how patient you are with me.
Amen.

Creativity and Laughter

Dear God, give me eyes to see the humor in religion.
Give me ears to hear what is funny, amusing,
or downright hilarious.
Help me to share the bubble of laughter
rising in me with my community of faith.
And God? Remind me to smile often in my faith community.
Amen.

Courage

Dear God, give me courage for this day,
just this one day, because I will speak to you again tomorrow.
Help me remember that you are always with me,
that you care about me,
and that you love me no matter how badly I mess up.
And God? Remind me that you will always hold my hand.
Amen.

Busyness

Dear God, slow me down.
Sit me down and have a cup of tea with me.
Remind me to breathe deeply and slowly
and to bless this day that is holy
like all the other days of my life.
And God? Thanks for always being there.
Amen.

Meditation on Gifts

Now there are varieties of gifts, but the same Spirit
(1 Cor 12:4).

I am a person with gifts.

Sometimes it is hard for me to believe these gifts are mine,
that the Spirit of life lives uniquely through me
through this unique contribution of abilities and qualities.

I notice that some people have the gift of speaking well and
clearly in groups; other people organize events and follow
through thoroughly to the end.

My friends are healers and cleaners, musicians and writers,
drivers and supervisors, builders and artists.

I am many things, and I am a minister.

Someone might say to me, "You are a minister.
You have chosen to spend some time and energy,
some thought, and some care to help others grow in faith."
I would listen if someone told me that.

I choose to be a minister, and that matters to me.
Sometimes I believe that it matters to God,
and sometimes I am not sure that it does.
My contribution does not seem like a lot.

I listen to what Paul wrote in his letters to the people in
Corinth:

There are varieties of gifts, … but it is the same God
who activates all of them in everyone.

It changes what I do and what I say.

Everything I do could make a difference, God's difference.
Everything I say could have an ear, God's ear.

Thank you, God, for these gifts.

Thank you, God, for your opportunities.

Thank you, God, for your Spirit.

Prayers with Groups

Prayer Scrapbook

If the group members are taking turns leading the opening prayer, create a prayer scrapbook. Include any prayers listed here or any that the group members find or write.

Teach Us, O God

Teach us, O God, to follow your way:
to give and not count the cost;
to risk and not heed the wounds;
to toil and not seek for rest;
to labor and not ask for reward;
to live and love as Jesus taught us.
Amen.

Open Our Hearts and Minds

O God,
open our ears to hear what you are saying to us in the things that happen to us and in the people we meet.
Open our eyes to see the needs of people around us.
Open our hands to do our work well
and help where help is needed.
Open our lips to bring comfort, joy, and laughter to other people and to share your good news.
Open our minds to discover new truths
about you and our world.
Open our hearts to love you and our neighbors
as you have loved us.
Amen.

Jesus Blessing

May the Jesus Christ
who walks on wounded feet
walk with you to the end of the road.
May the Jesus Christ
who serves with wounded hands
help you to serve one another.
May the Jesus Christ
who loves with a wounded heart
be your love forever.
Bless God wherever you go,
and may you see the face of Jesus
in everyone you meet.

Litanies

In a litany prayer, a leader reads a sentence or a phrase, and the group responds with a phrase that is repeated throughout the prayer. Litanies can be prayers of praise, confession, thanksgiving, or supplication. The prayer of the faithful, used for both Eucharist and Liturgy of the Hours, is a litany prayer. They are easy to write in a group situation.

List things you are thankful for, sorry for, or have concerns about on newsprint. Resist the temptation to preach with complicated "that" phrases. Pray "for" people. Thank God "for" gifts. Then discuss and decide on a short responsive phrase. Write the response on a separate sheet. A lead-in phrase, such as "Let us pray," can clue the group to respond.

Circle Prayer

Invite the group to stand in a circle holding hands. Explain that you will begin with a simple sentence prayer and then squeeze the hand of the person to your right. That person will then offer a sentence prayer aloud or silently to God and then squeezes the hand of the person to the right. When the squeeze returns to the leader, conclude the prayer.

International Peace Prayer

Lead me from death to life, from falsehood to truth.
Lead me from despair to hope, from fear to trust.
Lead me from hate to love, from war to peace.
Let peace fill our hearts, our world, our universe.

Closing Prayer

May the light of God surround us,
the love of God enfold us,
the power of God protect us,
the presence of God watch over us,
and the spirit of God dwell in us. Amen.

Commissioning

Go forth now, into a world
in which apathy and half-heartedness are dominant.
Move the world a little for God's sake.

Liturgy of the Hours

Whenever the church community gathers, morning and evening prayer is always appropriate. Vatican Council II restored the Liturgy of the Hours to daily communal prayer. By offering praise to God through the Hours, we consecrate the day and night and join with Christ in unceasing prayer. From the simple format below, choose a prayer for the time of day your group comes together. You may offer the first part of the prayer as the Gathering prayer for a group and the remainder for a Missioning prayer. The natural break comes after the psalm, and the "Scripture" for the prayer can be a reading from the liturgy for that week. The prayer for Missioning begins with the Benedictus or Magnificat. Praying the entire prayer for Gathering or Missioning is another option.

Keep the hymns simple so everyone feels comfortable joining in. If possible, invite a music minister to lead the singing.

The Liturgy of the Hours offers the world vigilant prayer. The tradition ensures that the church never ceases to pray as members offer prayer from time zone to time zone. Pray a version of morning or evening prayer with your group. The following easy format will help guide you, or use the morning and evening prayer books that many publishers offer.

For Morning Prayer

Opening Prayer: *Everyone makes the sign of the cross on their lips. Light a candle or candles.*

Leader: O God, open our lips.

All: So that all may proclaim your praise.

Hymn of Praise: *Pray or sing one of the following psalm options together, alternating sides for alternate verses.*

   Ordinary Time: Psalm 99, 63, or 5
   Lent: Psalm 51 or 30
   Easter: Psalm 92 or 149
   Advent–Christmas: Psalm 67 or 96

Scripture Reading: *One member proclaims a Scripture reading of the day. The group may choose a book of the Bible and read a few verses.*

Gospel Canticle — Benedictus: *Say together the Canticle of Zechariah, Luke 1:68–79.*

Prayer Petitions: *While praising our benevolent God, pray for the needs of the world, for those we remember in prayer, and for the work of the day. End with the Lord's Prayer.*

Concluding Prayer

Leader: O God,
   let your Spirit come on us to guide us through this day.
   Let the words we speak and the things we do
   give glory to you alone.
   May Jesus be our model,
   and guide us in Christ so all things are made right.

Blessing

Leader: May God bless us and keep us in divine care.

Dismissal

Leader: We go forth in the name of the Father, and of the Son, and of the Holy Spirit.

All: Amen.

For Evening Prayer

Opening Prayer: *Everyone makes the sign of the cross. While lighting a candle or candles, the leader begins as follows:*

Leader: Jesus Christ is the light of the world.

All: A light that no shadow can overpower.

Hymn: *Sing a short and well-known hymn that acclaims Christ as the light of the world.*

Incense: *Pause for a moment to enjoy the candlelight as a symbol of Christ's presence, and then light the incense.*

Leader: Let our prayer rise like incense.

All: As we offer an evening oblation.

Psalm: *Sing or pray one of the following psalm options together, alternating sides for alternate verses.*

> **Ordinary Time:** Psalm 15, 41, or 141
> **Lent:** Psalm 28 or 116
> **Easter:** Psalm 100 or 113
> **Advent–Christmas:** Psalm 24 or 132

Scripture Reading: *One member proclaims a Scripture reading of the day. The group may choose a book of the Bible and read a few verses.*

Gospel Canticle — Magnificat: *Say together the Canticle of Mary, Luke 1:46–55.*

Prayer Petitions: *Pray on behalf of the church, the world, the nation and community, the sick, and the dead. End with the Lord's Prayer.*

Concluding Prayer: *After praying the Lord's Prayer together, the leader asks for a blessing, and the group responds "Amen." The prayer concludes with the sign of peace.*

Leader: O God, free us from the powers of darkness. Protect us through this night, that we may rise in safety to live in your light.

Blessing

Leader: May God bless us and keep us in divine care.

Dismissal

Leader: We go forth in the name of the Father, and of the Son, and of the Holy Spirit.

All: Amen.

Group-Building Activities / Icebreakers

Balloon Messages

Have the members write their names on slips of paper and include one of their favorite things. Each person folds the paper, puts it in a balloon, blows up the balloon, ties it, and puts it in the center of the circle. Then everyone chooses a balloon, pops it, and reads the message. Each person finally finds and introduces that person — and his or her favorite thing — to the group.

Alphabetical Name Line-Up

Ask the participants to line up alphabetically by first name without speaking. For members who are new to one another, nametags will be helpful.

Birthday Line-Up

Ask the group to line up in the order of their birthdays, starting with today's date. When they form the line, use it to talk about who has birthdays soon, around Christmas, in the summer, and so on. Ask, "When is the best time to have a birthday?"

G.O.B.W.E.O.

"**G**etting **o**n **B**oard **w**ith **E**ach **O**ther" is a quick way to see how everyone is doing before moving into a session. Ask, "What was good about your week, and what was not so good?" Going around the circle, each person in turn "checks in" with a response. No one comments or asks for additional information at this time. This is a time for listening.

Chain Interview

Set up chairs facing each other in two circles, one chair for each person in the group. Prepare fifteen to twenty questions about personal preferences, family and home, world concerns, careers, and why they came. After you ask the first question, everyone moves one seat to the right. New partners face each other and ask a new question. Everyone finds out a little about the others.

Ministry Sign-In

Adapt the following statements to relate to the interests and activities of your community. Make copies of a list with a space to sign after each. Have the members circulate and have others "sign in" where appropriate.

- I am on the social justice committee.
- I am artistic.
- I am a minister of the word.
- I am currently raising children.
- I am a hospitality minister.
- I bake bread.
- My grandparents were members of this community.
- I am a new member of this faith community.
- I usually worship on Saturday evening.
- I am a catechist for children.
- I am glad to be here.
- I enjoy singing liturgical music.
- I pray morning and evening prayer.
- I was confirmed as a young child.
- I was confirmed as an adult.

Human Knots

Up to twelve people stand in a circle. Have everyone reach across the circle and join hands with two different people (but not with the people on either side or both hands of the same person). By stepping over and ducking under arms, slowly untie this human knot. Ask them not to drop hands but to let hands rotate as they need to. Sometimes you will form two circles depending on how the hands were joined. Celebrate your cooperative achievement! This is a visual experience of what God wants for our world. When the group is untangled, discuss the following:

- How did you get started?
- What problems did you have?
- How did you feel?
- What did you learn?

Island in the Sun

Tape five pieces of newsprint to the floor to represent islands. Have everyone choose an "island" on which to "sun." Play Caribbean or Hawaiian music, and encourage people to cruise around and visit other islands. If you want to jazz this up, bring sunglasses and sun hats for everyone to wear. While they wander around and greet one another, remove one of the islands. When the music stops, they all seek an island on which to sun. At least one foot must be on the island. Continue this process, removing one island each time, until everyone is together "sunning" on the same island. Celebrate your togetherness! Remember to support one another so no one falls off and drowns. Point out that we were created to live in community and support one another.

Either-Or Exercise

This exercise encourages personal connection, imagination, and symbolic thinking. Choose a Bible story, and develop either-or questions. The following are examples:

- Who are you more like: the prodigal son or the older brother?
- What would you be more likely to spend your inheritance on: a car or a party for your friends?
- Is this a happy story or a sad story?

Clear the room so people can move easily. Ask a question that has two clear alternatives, inviting those who choose the first option to go to one side of the room and those who choose the second option to go to the other side. Encourage people to go with their first impulses and not spend too much time thinking. After the exercise, return to the center of the room and discuss using the following:

- Was it easy or difficult to decide?
- Were you ever almost alone on one side of the room? How did that feel?
- Who else seemed to make the same choices you did?
- How did that feel?

Continuum Exercise

This is a variant of the "Either-Or Exercise." Label one end of the room "Agree" and the other "Disagree." People can place themselves anywhere along a line, including right in the middle if they are neutral, to indicate how they feel about something. Read aloud an opinion statement (such as "I love Brussels sprouts," "I think women should be able to be deacons," "I think violent movies should be banned," or "I believe immigration laws should be revised"). Ask the participants to place themselves on a line from "very strongly agree" to "very strongly disagree." Use a variety of statements — some silly, some serious — and at the end, invite everyone to talk about reasons behind their opinions.

Department Store Game

Ask the participants to imagine that they are in a department store that contains all the possible human traits (wisdom, laziness, understanding, impatience). One by one, ask them to share a trait they would like to "buy" from the store and one trait they already possess that they would like to "return" to the store.

Values Auction

This game helps players identify basic societal values represented by the different items in the auction. They can see how their choices illustrate their own values.

- Make paper money or use play money. Each participant receives $5,000 to spend at the auction.
- Make an auction sheet by listing the things you plan to auction. Adapt the sample list to the group participating in this activity. Give a copy of the auction list and a pencil to each participant.
- Ask each person to decide what to bid on and mark his or her sheet.
- Auction off each item. The auctioneer should be lively and keep things moving along.
- After the auction, display newsprint sheets with the following values listed: justice, power, fame, love, achievement, physical attractiveness, and others. Discuss the following:
    What values do your purchases represent?
    Did you have to give up one thing to get something else?
    In our group, what seemed to be the most important values, judged by those things that people competed to buy?

Sample Auction List

1. Rid the world of racism.
2. Be voted the "Outstanding Person of the Year."
3. Take a trip to the destination of your choice.
4. Appear in a movie with your favorite star.
5. Understand the meaning of life.
6. Become the richest person in the world.
7. Be the most powerful person in the world.
8. Lead a social justice movement.
9. Have the house of your dreams.
10. Win the "Most Valuable Player" award in a professional sport of your choice.
11. Establish world peace.

All Souls Day Prayer

Before the prayer service, invite the participants and families from the faith community to set up *altarcitos* — that is, little altars that commemorate deceased loved ones. Set up tables around the perimeter of the room to which people can add photographs and memorabilia of deceased family members. As they gather they circulate around the room and view the *altarcitos.* Distribute Bibles or words/music.

Sing: "You Are Near" or "Pescador De Hombres" from *Breaking Bread*

O God, you give us marvelous companions
on our journey home to you.
They teach us about your love and goodness
and share your call to holiness and wholeness.
Help us to respond wholeheartedly and know the joy
of sharing with others what we receive:
faith and love in the name of Jesus.
Amen.

Substitute or add other readings from the Masses for the two feasts.

First Reading: Hebrews 12:1–2

Responsorial:
These are the people who long to see God's face.

Use Bibles to pray Psalm 24:1–6, alternating verses and saying the response after each.

Gospel: John 11:21–27

Have a storyteller tell a marvelous story about the dead, or use the following reflection.

Reflection

Invite the participants to relax, breathe deeply, close their eyes, and breathe deeply again.

Quiet yourself. Focus on those people who are your models of faith. (*Pause.*) Choose one person. Imagine that person's face smiling in front of you. (*Pause.*) What is that person telling you at this time? (*Pause.*) What are you missing, something that this person can see? (*Pause.*) In your mind visualize that person giving you something. (*Pause.*) Focus more clearly. What does the person hand to you? (*Pause.*) Your friend is saying something to you. What words of encouragement do you hear? (*Pause.*) What is something very important you would like to tell this friend in faith? Tell the person now. (*Pause.*) Thank your friend and say goodbye for now. (*Pause.*) Thank God for sending this person into your life. (*Pause.*) When you are ready, open your eyes and return to this place.

Invite the group with litanies, if there are any, to read them aloud.

Closing

Loving Creator, thank you for people in our lives
who were and are our companions in faith.
Keep us always in the communion of your saints,
and guide us in being instruments of your peace.
Help us bring others to know and love you
as others helped us.
We ask all these gifts through Jesus, your Son,
in whom we pray and who lives with you and the Spirit.
Amen.

Sing: "Blessed Feasts Of Blessed Martyrs" or "I Will Not Die" from *Breaking Bread*

Gather together for supper if it will be served. Have the group with Day of the Dead treats serve them now or with supper.

Minister's Prayer

Loving Creator,
Jesus our companion, Spirit of love,
into your care we place
our gifts and talents, our experiences,
our work of preparation,
and our desire to do your will.

Take these gifts and transform them
into the wisdom, love, and courage
that we need to serve your beloved ones.

In times of difficulty, help us remember
that we live, move, and have our being in you.
You chose us and entrust us to be here now,
and that is good.

Blessed Mother,
strengthen our yes with your conviction.
Accompany us in times of doubt,
so that we might never despair.

Grant that we may be signs and messengers
of divine love in all we do
and to all those we touch today.
Amen.

Loving Creator,
Jesus our companion, Spirit of love,
into your care we place
our gifts and talents, our experiences,
our work of preparation,
and our desire to do your will.

Take these gifts and transform them
into the wisdom, love, and courage
that we need to serve your beloved ones.

In times of difficulty, help us remember
that we live, move, and have our being in you.
You chose us and entrust us to be here now,
and that is good.

Blessed Mother,
strengthen our yes with your conviction.
Accompany us in times of doubt,
so that we might never despair.

Grant that we may be signs and messengers
of divine love in all we do
and to all those we touch today.
Amen.

Loving Creator,
Jesus our companion, Spirit of love,
into your care we place
our gifts and talents, our experiences,
our work of preparation,
and our desire to do your will.

Take these gifts and transform them
into the wisdom, love, and courage
that we need to serve your beloved ones.

In times of difficulty, help us remember
that we live, move, and have our being in you.
You chose us and entrust us to be here now,
and that is good.

Blessed Mother,
strengthen our yes with your conviction.
Accompany us in times of doubt,
so that we might never despair.

Grant that we may be signs and messengers
of divine love in all we do
and to all those we touch today.
Amen.

Loving Creator,
Jesus our companion, Spirit of love,
into your care we place
our gifts and talents, our experiences,
our work of preparation,
and our desire to do your will.

Take these gifts and transform them
into the wisdom, love, and courage
that we need to serve your beloved ones.

In times of difficulty, help us remember
that we live, move, and have our being in you.
You chose us and entrust us to be here now,
and that is good.

Blessed Mother,
strengthen our yes with your conviction.
Accompany us in times of doubt,
so that we might never despair.

Grant that we may be signs and messengers
of divine love in all we do
and to all those we touch today.
Amen.

Family Healing Prayer

Redeeming God, look on your people with mercy.

In your loving kindness, heal all that has been hurt

through thoughtless words and deeds.

Re-love into wholeness the fractured,

fragmented parts of your people.

Re-create them to be who you have purposed them to be.

Re-establish deep within them their identity as your children,

created in your image.

We ask you, O Jesus,

to heal the family tree of each of us gathered here.

We pray that through the power of your Holy Spirit,

all chaos created by sin, all blurred and misguided vision,

and all rebelliousness that has manifested itself

in many ways will be healed.

We pray that all distress in the family tree

be calmed by your love.

We pray that those gathered today

might experience in new ways

your gifts of freedom and peace.

One God forever. Amen.

Bilingual Prayers for Lent and Pentecost

LENT

Ten Piedad de Nosotros / Have Mercy on Us

Cristo, óyenos.
Jesus Christ, pray for us.

Dios en celestial, que quieres que todos seamos hermanos.
Ten piedad de nosotros.

Heavenly God, you call us to be one family.
Have mercy on us.

Jesucristo, liberador del peado y de sus consecuencias.
Ten piedad de nosotros.

Christ Jesus, you free us from sin and all its effects.
Have mercy on us.

Dios Espiritu Santo,
animador de la iglesia y renovador de la faz de la tierra.
Ten piedad de nosotros.

Holy Spirit of God,
guide your church and renew the face of the earth.
Have mercy on us.

Dios Justo y Misericordioso / God of Justice and Mercy

Los grupos alternos para cada verso.
Alternate groups for each verse.

Te damos gracias, Dios santo, Dios justo y misericordioso,
Porque la esperanza que en ti ponen
los pobres no has sido ni será defraudada.

God of justice and mercy, the poor have hope in you,
and they shall not be disappointed.

Tú eres la fuerza de los débiles,
eres el Dios liberador, el Dios que salva.

You, O holy One, are the power for all who are weak.
You are the liberating God, the God who saves.

PENTECOST

Nosotros Somos Su Pueblo / We Are God's people

Nosotros somos su pueblo.
We are God's people.

Nosotros somos ovejas de su rebaño.
We are the sheep of God's flock.

Te alabamos gracias, Dios.
We praise you, God.

Te alabamos gracias y te bendecimos, Dios.
We praise you and bless you, God.

O Dios, tus obras son admirables.
Your works, O God, are wonderful.

Tú tienes las palabras de vida eterna.
You have the words of everlasting life.

Amen.

Dios Te Acompañana / God Goes with You

Todos están parados en un círculo. Diga a la persona próxima hasta que cada uno recibe el mensaje:

"Te acompañan Dios y todos los angeles."

All stand in a circle. Say the following to the next person until everyone receives the message:

"God goes with you, God and all the angels."

Amen.

Ongoing Evaluation Form

1. What were my strengths during this group experience?

2. Is there something I can try to do differently next time?

3. To whom could I turn for help or mentoring, or how could I mentor someone else?

4. How have the gifts and needs of the participants been incorporated into the process?

5. How did I involve the participants' families and other faith community members?

6. How are the members called to deepen their spirituality and to serve others?

7. Did I allow enough time for an unhurried prayer experience?

8. How did I encourage the building of community?

9. How will I and those who were with me act more justly?

10. How did the Spirit move among the group members?